Information include my knowledge. When possible, court documents, legal briefs, etc., have been obtained to corroborate the specific details being quoted and described. When necessary, paraphrases of conversations are used; they are intended to capture the most accurate and authentic spirit of what was said and done, based on my observations and personal recollections.

I am not an informant. All names mentioned are part of the official record, recounted here not to accuse but to demonstrate the vast array of suspects, divergent theories, and conflicting statements that emerged in the aftermath of the uprising.

For more information, go to www.keithlamar.org.

Table of Contents

In loving memory of my aunt,
Harriet Brooks, who walked through
the valley of the shadow of death
and refused to fear the evil.
May God have mercy on your soul.

Foreword
by Denis O'Hearn

I never expected to work with prisoners. Then one day I got a letter from Keith LaMar. He had read my biography of the Irish hunger striker, Bobby Sands, and he wanted to correspond with the author. Like many other prisoners across the world, he had seen something special in the spirit of Bobby Sands, and I think he wanted somehow to hold onto that spirit and maybe learn more about it. We started writing to each other. Then he asked me to visit him. In a few short years he has become my brother. Indeed, I tell him things that I would never reveal to my genetic brother, the other closest man in my life.

I approached my first visit with Keith (or Bomani, the name he adopted as he prepared for trial on charges emerging from the Lucasville Uprising) with some trepidation. Because he is a long-term prisoner, and since I was coming from out-of-state, we were allowed a six-hour visit on Saturday and then again on Sunday. What in god's name would you talk about for such a long time? I knew I wouldn't be able to leave him even a minute early, to be taken back to that bleak isolation cell. Each second was a gift, I reasoned.

I was also warned about the conditions. He would be chained and handcuffed in a tiny locked room. I would sit in a small room across from him, with two thick panes of bulletproof glass between us. To be heard, we would have to yell at each other. And since he was not allowed out of his room for food or a drink, or to use the toilet, I would have to remain with him out of solidarity. Regardless of what my stomach or my bladder said to me, I could not take advantage of something he could not also have.

I shouldn't have worried. For several years, until Bomani and three of his comrades won the right to semi-contact visits through a successful 2011 hunger strike, I tried to visit him once a month. During all that time, the conversation never flagged. Not that I am such a great conversationalist; no, it was because Bomani is one of the most engaging men you will ever talk to. I soon realized that each second was indeed a gift, but Bomani was the giver and *I* was on the receiving end.

Since then, I have visited a number of other men in supermax prisons and I have found that they can all keep up both sides of a conversation. You see, they have no human contact within the prison and often no one with whom they can have an intelligent conversation through the cell door. On a visit, it all comes flowing out.

Once I asked Bomani if he ever had any good conversations with the other men in his pod.

"Well, I did have one conversation yesterday," he began. "There is this one dude in the pod—a white dude. I can just see him out of my window and sometimes I'll catch him looking at me, staring at me to see what I am doing. A couple of days ago, he saw me reading and after a while he asked me what I was reading. I told him. Then he said that he was reading a book by a man called Hitler, a book called *Mein Kampf*. He said this Hitler had some really good ideas about racial purity and the Jews. 'But don't you think he went a bit too far?' I asked. 'No,' he said, 'in my opinion he didn't go far enough!'"

The point, as became clear after we talked about it, was that this was a *good* conversation. Repugnant as it was, at least it had some kind of intellectual content! Mostly, the men in the pod just talk shit and few of them have any formal education or do any reading at all. Sometimes they bug out and they scream and moan. This is what passes for intellectual discourse in supermax. So it is no small wonder that a well-read and thoughtful man like Bomani would relish the chance to talk to someone from the outside world, about things that hardly ever come up in his everyday life.

What *is* surprising, though, is the level of Keith LaMar's intellectual engagement. Not only is he one of the better read people I have ever come across—he literally devours whatever books he can get his hands on, whether it be literature or poetry—he has two remarkable talents. One is his retention of things, his wonderful memory. Quote him a line from a poem and he somehow tracks it down, memorizes it, and quotes back the whole thing to you on a subsequent visit. The other is his ability to read something, to see what is good about it, and then to incorporate that into his own writing without the result simply being derivative or copycat. Over his years in prison he has found his own voice, albeit a voice that constantly learns from others and expands.

And what a voice it is.

Here, in this account of his treatment after the Lucasville Uprising of 1993, you will find a compelling defense against the capital condemnation he has endured at the hands of a system that is not just broken, but actively *made* not to work. It is a system that is twisted by public officials who are corrupt, prejudiced, often vindictive, and sometimes just lazy; by scared men who are willing to sacrifice others so that they may survive those prejudices and corruptions; and by a scared public that has become convinced we will be safer if we can just lock up more men and throw away the keys.

And when Keith LaMar demonstrates this prejudice by telling his story, it is not only or even primarily race he is talking about. Race is a part of it: he was condemned partly because he is a black man from East Cleveland in the United States of America. Yet two of the other men who face death sentences after stage-managed trials following the Lucasville Uprising are white. The uprising itself was remarkable because it *transcended* race. Whites and black nationalists came out in solidarity with their Sunni Muslim brothers. During the uprising they made signs and scribbled messages on the prison walls: *Convict Race* and *Black and White Together*. Recently, hunger strikers in the Security Housing Unit (SHU) of Pelican Bay showed the same leadership when they persuaded the prisoners in general population to put an end to all racial and gang violence in California's prisons. This was followed by the formation of a Youth Justice Coalition among young gang leaders in Los Angeles, who agreed to follow the lead from SHU prisoners in Pelican Bay and to "end all the killing and drama between hoods, crews, and races."

No, the primary prejudice that Keith LaMar got caught up in is against the poor. We live in a society that no longer has any use for the poor, that no longer has jobs for them and no longer wants to help pay for their upkeep as free men and women. As the sociologist Loic Wacquant puts it, we are a society that "punishes the poor" *because* they are poor. And Keith LaMar is only one of the many victims of that social process.

I use the word victim advisedly, because in all the years I have known him, Bomani has never acted like a victim or claimed to be a victim. Sure, he goes through periods of depression. But wouldn't anyone if he were kept in solitary confinement for 19 years, unable to touch any human or other living thing... or to be touched? Going to bed and waking every day with the knowledge that the State wants to kill him?

What is remarkable about Bomani is his resilience, his insistence that he must do something righteous with whatever he has left of his life. He wants to say something to young people that keeps them from following the path he chose. He wants to say something to his fellow inmates that will shake them out of their destructive ways, that will impel them to seek meaning in their lives, even in supermax prison.

Bomani often tells me that he does not regret his time in Ohio State Penitentiary, because there he found himself. Only problem is, once a man truly finds himself, he must be true to himself. He must find a way to control his own destiny even though prison guards and the forces of the State want to control him. A man who really finds himself must be brutally honest, most of all to himself: he will not lie and he will not incriminate another human being to save himself. If he did, he could not look himself in the eye.

That is why Keith LaMar faces execution.

Have we not gone astray somewhere, sometime? Do we really want to live in a society where someone who lies to save himself can find mercy but the same man is condemned if he insists on telling the truth, especially if he maintains his innocence even though he knows he may die because of it?

I have this vague memory of my father saying to me as a child, "Always tell the truth, son, even when it is hard to do so, even when a lie is the easy way out. When you tell the truth, you are being true to yourself."

But in the United States we have a "justice" system that tells us, "lie... blame the other guy... you can get off... just cop a plea...."

Keith LaMar listened to the first voice, the voice I remember from my father. He found that voice even though he never even had a father. He found it through snippets of relationships with prisoners who showed him kindness and solidarity. Somehow this remarkable man found a strength and a truth within himself. As I said, he can read a book or a poem and see what is good about it, and he can incorporate that goodness into his own writing without being derivative, without just being a copycat. Well, it seems that he has also learned, somehow, to observe life and to see what is good about it; and he can incorporate that goodness into his own life and actions. I don't know what he did or who he was when he was 18, or even 23. I have an inkling who he was because he speaks honestly, though regretfully, about what he did and the choices he made.

But I know who Keith LaMar is now. I believe he is innocent of the charges for which he faces execution.

In this book, he tells a compelling story. And he leaves us with the burning question: *Why would a man insist on his innocence when he knows that all he has to do to save his life is to plead guilty?* I can only find one reasonable answer to such a question: *because he is innocent and because he is true to himself and simply cannot say otherwise.*

But, to me, all this talk of guilt and innocence is only secondary in the end. The important thing I know is that Keith LaMar is precious. His is a genuine voice, the voice of a *natural* intellectual, not one of those manufactured intellectuals like me, who populate our universities. In a society such as we live in today, can we afford to lose such men or women, those who have such potential to make this world a better place? Surely, we don't have enough of them. Let us hold onto him... tightly. We cannot let him slip away.

—*Denis O'Hearn, Istanbul, Turkey, June 2013*

Into the furnace let me go alone;
Stay you without in terror of the heat.
I will go naked in—for thus 'tis sweet—
Into the weird depths of the hottest zone.
I will not quiver in the frailest bone,
You will not note a flicker of defeat;
My heart shall tremble not its fate to meet,
My mouth give utterance to any moan.
The yawning oven spits forth fiery spears;
Red aspish tongues shout wordlessly my name.
Desire destroys, consumes my mortal fears,
Transforming me into a shape of flame.
I will come out, back to your world of tears,
A stronger soul within a finer frame.

Baptism by Claude McKay

Sketch by Claude Meyer

Condemned
the whole story

Lucasville: A Brief History

Based on the official account, the Lucasville Prison Uprising arose out of a dispute between the warden and a group of Sunni Muslim inmates who refused to take a mandatory tuberculosis test. According to the Muslims, the serum that was being used to determine whether or not inmates were infected contained an alcoholic substance called phenol, which, based on Islamic doctrine, they were prohibited from ingesting.

In an attempt to resolve this dilemma, several Muslim leaders met with the warden and other members of the administration. There was an intense exchange that ultimately resulted in a stalemate. The following was drafted by Imam Siddique Abdullah Hasan based on his recollection of what occurred:[1]

[Warden] Tate: Sanders [aka Hasan], do you have anything to say?

Hasan: I have nothing to say. You have already said what is going to happen and I see no reason to waste my breath.

Tate: This is a meeting. I want to hear what you have to say.

Hasan: This is not a meeting where what we say

---

[1] Staughton Lynd, *Lucasville: The Untold Story of a Prison Uprising* (PM Press, 2d ed., 2011), pages 25-26.

makes a difference. It is a meeting where you are being a dictator, and have adopted a hardline approach. You are not being sensitive in understanding our leadership position on the test.

Tate: Elmore [Taymullah, a fellow Muslim inmate in attendance], what do you have to say?

Taymullah: The test is unlawful for us to take. We have no intention of taking it, for we would be guilty of a sin. However, if someone forces us to take the test, we will be absolved of the sin.

Chaplain Lewis [smilingly]: How much force would have to be applied in order for you to be absolved of the sin?

Taymullah: This is not a joking matter. The bottom line is we are not going to take the test.

Tate: Elmore, what will you do if one of my officers grabs you and tries to give you the test?

Taymullah: I can't say what I will do. You do what you have to do and we will do what we have to do.

Namir [aka James Were, a fellow Muslim inmate in attendance]: I do not trust the prison officials to test us. You have the reputation for using us as guinea pigs.

Tate: Mr. Roddy [deputy warden], when will you finish testing the inmates that are HIV positive?

Roddy: By Friday, April 9.

Tate: Then we will be ready to start testing you early next week. I hope you will change your minds.

According to Hasan, "The vibes were somewhat tense" when they got up to leave this meeting. On Wednesday, April 7, Hasan sent the warden the following message:

> In spite of what the modernist and Westernized Muslims say, the TB substance is unlawful for a Muslim and an infringement on his right.
> A person can be tested positive or negative by taking an X-ray test and/or spitting into a cup. Hence, we have no legal objections to this form of testing and pray to the Most High that you and your staff will accommodate us in this form of TB testing.
> In closing, I was informed that the above optional policy was instituted at Mansfield Correctional Institution.
> We thank you in advance for your time, consideration and mutual cooperation in being of any assistance to the Muslim body here.
> We anxiously await your response.

In the scheme of things, this was not an unreasonable request. Indeed, it was standard practice that such religious observances were accommodated so long as they were verifiable. To that end, Muslim leaders came to this meeting with a letter from Islamic authorities in Port Elizabeth, South Africa, that supported their refusal to ingest phenol. However, instead of bending to meet the Muslims where they stood, Warden Tate chose to impose his will:

I believe you realize that I have the utmost respect both for you personally and for your religious beliefs.

Your position relative to TB testing is, however, one that is not rational nor will it be accepted by me. Your options have been explained and I expect full compliance to my orders for all SOCF inmates to be tested. There will be no deviations to this order.

I trust you, as well others who feel as you do, will comply with this policy. You are in no position to dictate to me how you perceive this should occur. I am certainly hoping there will be minimal difficulties associated with this process.

On Good Friday, April 9, a day after issuing this thinly-veiled threat, Warden Tate left the facility for the weekend without raising the alarm about the tenuous state of things. When word leaked out from the kitchen that an order for 3,500 brown-bag lunches had been made, the Muslims were tipped off that a lockdown was planned for that Monday, April 12, forcing them to hurriedly respond. On Sunday, April 11, the Muslims embarked on what they hoped would be a peaceful protest. Yet, failing to take into account the explosive atmosphere that prevailed inside the prison, the protest quickly erupted into a bloody, 11-day ordeal during which nine inmates and one correctional officer were killed. But this is only part of the story. In fact, what happened on April 11, 1993, was a long time coming.

The Southern Ohio Correctional Facility (commonly called "Lucasville") is located in Lucasville, Ohio, a virtually all-white city in the southernmost part of the state. A town divested of its mills and factories by 1993, Lucasville followed in the tradition of the typical rural prison where mostly poor, white citizens watched over predominantly black prisoners from the inner city. As one might imagine, it was a place rife with racism, where white guards openly flaunted racist tattoos such as Nazi swastikas and lightning bolts. In terms of race relations, it was steeped in down-home sensibilities, where the word "nigger" was commonly uttered and the casual word or glance misdirected at a white woman could easily result in an Emmett Till-style beating or death.

In 1990, three years before the uprising, a black inmate viciously murdered a white schoolteacher by the name of Beverly Taylor. Allegedly, after a botched rape attempt that turned into a hostage situation, the inmate panicked and cut Ms. Taylor's throat, violently ending her life. The reaction in the surrounding community was at once vengeful and deafening: "Kill him!"

They wanted the inmate to be put to death. Indeed, according to those who were at the prison at the time, a kind of vigilante justice set in and guards beat the inmate to within an inch of his life. But somehow he survived and a trial was had.

As expected, the inmate was found guilty but, because of his diminished mental capacity, was barred from receiving the death penalty. Not surprisingly, this reignited the anger among the guards and those in the community and they, together, began calling for the complete lockdown of the prison.

Eventually, amid a cacophony of hate, a new warden was appointed. His name was Arthur Tate. He was chosen because of his "tough-on-prisoners" attitude and, in keeping with his reputation, immediately instituted a series of new rules that were supposedly designed to restore order. For example, he had yellow lines painted on each side of the corridors and inmates were directed to stay within these lines as they walked to and fro throughout the prison. He also began enforcing a strict dress code mandating that inmates keep their shirts tucked in at all times. To curtail movement, he cut programs and severely limited out-of-cell time.

Still, as tough as he was or tried to be, he could only do so much. Although Lucasville was designated a maximum-security prison, it was impossible for Warden Tate to completely lock the penitentiary down as those in the surrounding community demanded. Before long, he came under fire and was accused of coddling inmates, a perception that he despised and sought to dispel by seeking to build a separate high-security lockup on the grounds of the prison.

Plans were drawn up and presented to Eric Dahlberg, South Regional Director of the Ohio Department of Rehabilitation and Correction, for approval. Had anyone been paying attention to the trends regarding prison construction, this would have provided the first hint of things to come. At the time, "supermax" prisons (as they would come to be known) were being built all across the country, and Ohio was late in the race to erect its first ultra-modern, high-tech penitentiary. Perhaps this is what Warden Tate had in mind? If so, his plans were put on hold after funds sought from the state legislature were denied. As it turned out, Lucasville already had a high-security unit that consisted of 20 cells, which were seldom used. How, then, to justify such a costly expenditure of taxpayers' money?

"If you ever want to know what something was about," suggests Noam Chomsky, "look at the changes it produced."

When one looks back on the events that preceded the uprising, the only conclusion that can be reached is that it was provoked in order to create the justification for the building of Ohio's first supermax prison. In order to demonstrate that 20 cells were not enough to contain the "potential violence" that Warden Tate predicted, a disturbance was needed that exceeded their capacity to control. They needed a riot.

Thus, with the kind of deliberateness that accompanies a strategy, Warden Tate began what became known as "Operation Shakedown." As simple as if flicking a switch, he gave his officers the green light to do whatever they wanted to do, thereby unleashing years of pent-up rage stemming from Beverly Taylor's death.

All of a sudden, minor transgressions were met with extreme hostility: if an inmate was caught crossing the yellow line in the corridors, it could result in him being slammed headfirst into the wall and then rushed to the hole to await disciplinary action. And this was only the beginning. To ratchet up the tension, known racists were forced into cells with their archenemies; highly coveted work assignments were summarily stripped away and given to those willing to become snitches, which, under the new regime, was made easier by the establishment of a post-office box to receive "anonymous" tips; cells were searched and trashed on an almost daily basis; new rules were created and then changed without notice, leaving inmates in a state of constant confusion; and just when one thought things could not get any worse, Mansfield Correctional Institution, a prison in northern Ohio, sent close to 300 of its most unruly inmates to Lucasville, creating a tinderbox of anger and fear. In the midst of all this volatility, the administration began showing ultra-violent prison movies depicting inmates stabbing, raping and killing each other.

As April approached, the tension in the air was flammable, and it was only a matter of time before a match was struck. Did Warden Tate, in sensing the overzealous commitment of the Muslims to obey their religious leaders, see a golden opportunity? In the meeting that occurred, he had to have noticed how agitated the Muslims were after he threatened to force them to take the TB tests. If, indeed, this was his intention, why did Warden Tate give the Muslims all weekend to plot a response?

These are questions that invite speculation. However, if it was Warden Tate's objective to initiate a disturbance, he played his hand to perfection. On April 11, 1993, when the Muslims stripped the guards of their keys and weapons and opened all the cell doors, years of repressed animosity burst forth in a torrent of unbridled aggression.

Warden Tate finally got his riot.

April 11, 1993:
Day of the Uprising

It was Easter Sunday and I was 23 years old, serving the fourth year of an 18 years-to-life sentence for murder. I had come to prison as a 19-year-old, still wet behind the ears and confounded by what seemed to be an extremely harsh punishment. Yes, I had taken someone's life, but I was not a "killer." I did not kill in cold blood, without remorse or without the requisite sorrow of someone who understands he has done something irrevocable.

Like most young men in the drug-infested neighborhood where I lived, I got caught up in the drug trade. The man I shot and killed was once my friend; we went to school together. However, by the time crack cocaine became an epidemic in 1988, we found ourselves playing opposing roles in a very twisted scene: I was the drug dealer and he was the dope fiend. He came to rob me and, as ridiculous as it may sound, I stood my ground. A shoot-out ensued. I shot him twice in the chest and, while attempting to run away, was shot twice in the legs by his accomplice. Under a hail of bullets, I managed to escape into the hallway of a nearby apartment building, where I promptly passed out. An ambulance was called. My friend and I arrived at the hospital together and lay next to each other in the operating room. He died and I was sent to prison, both of us only 19 years old.

For a long time I did not understand why I was the one who survived; it all seemed so random and meaningless. But coming so close to death made me open my eyes and realize how fragile life was. In the four years I had been in prison, I earned my GED and enrolled in the college program, trying, to the best of my ability, to redeem myself. I would make my life mean something, I vowed. And with the help of some very caring people, I put myself back on the path. I became a boxer (a very good one) and decided to fight for a second chance at life.

When I woke up on the morning of the uprising, I had no idea that the Muslims were having problems with the administration and had planned a protest. When the tuberculosis tests were administered a few weeks earlier, I had willingly submitted my arm to be poked and was relieved when, three days later, I learned that I did not have the disease. Word never reached me that the Muslims had refused to take the test. But had I known, I would have thought that it was none of my business, that it did not concern me. Little did I know, my whole life was about to change.

As holidays go in the penitentiary, the day started out slowly and quietly. The recreation yard had finally reopened after a long winter, and I was looking forward to clearing out my lungs. At 12:30 p.m., an announcement was made over the PA system that recreation had begun. I grabbed my gear and headed outside. I had made plans to meet up with one of my workout partners to do some "roadwork." The boxing season would be starting soon, and I wanted to be ready.

It was crowded on the track that afternoon: about 300 inmates came outside to catch the first whiff of spring. The sun was shining and the warmth from its rays loosened up my body.

"You think we can get 15 miles in?" my workout partner asked, looking doubtful. Neither of us was in the best of shape, but I felt good.

"Only one way to find out," I responded, smiling. With that, we took off jogging.

It took us almost the entire recreation period to jog 30 laps, the equivalent of 15 miles. *For a first attempt, that was decent,* I thought. It took a lot out of me, though; I was exhausted after we were done. At 2:45 p.m., the warning alarm sounded to alert us that it was time to start lining up to reenter the building. I took my place in line and waited.

As the line started moving forward, a guard came running out of the building with blood streaming down his face. Following him was a masked inmate who had somehow gotten ahold of the guard's nightstick and was now using it to beat him over the head.

"We takin' over!" the inmate screamed as he pummeled the guard.

I was shocked. Even though Lucasville was the most violent prison in Ohio, it was not every day that one witnessed an inmate attacking a guard; hence, we all stood back in stunned silence, watching in disbelief as the masked inmate repeatedly struck the guard in the head. It was a hell of a scene. And then, just as suddenly as it had started, it stopped. The guard, now bleeding profusely, collapsed to the ground and the inmate retreated inside the building.

"Can you believe this shit?" my workout partner asked.

I was too stunned to speak. *What the fuck is goin' on?* I wondered.

A few minutes later, several inmates wearing masks and carrying weapons appeared on the yard and announced that L-block was now under their control.

"We takin' over!" they repeated. "If any of y'all want to join us, come on in," they said, before withdrawing into the building. Though I was witnessing it with my own eyes, my mind was slow to accept what I was seeing.

Is this really happening? I asked myself.

As more and more inmates filtered out onto the yard, I retreated to a nearby picnic table with my workout partner to watch things unfold. Before long, word began to spread that cells were being robbed.

"You think we should go in?" I asked, thinking about my

personal property: clothes, shoes, television, radio, brand-new boxing boots, and so on. These things were my only worldly possessions and, with little to no help from home, had taken me years to acquire. Were they worth risking my life? The obvious answer is no. However, in that moment, the enormity of the situation had not yet fully registered. Yes, I saw the masked inmate beat the guard, and this fact alone should have given me pause. But surely the guards would regroup and restore order, right? In the meantime, what about my personal property? It never occurred to me that what I was witnessing was the beginning of an 11-day ordeal, or that, when all was said and done, I would be putting my life in jeopardy by going back inside.

As I sat there agonizing over what to do, my cellmate (a fellow boxer nicknamed "Blood Cunningham," who stayed in the cell when recreation was called) walked outside, leaving our personal belongings unguarded.

"What the fuck, Blood?" I asked, heading for the building. He was carrying his photo albums in his hand.

"Don't go in there, Keith," he warned me, with a crazed look on his face. "Mothafuckas done lost they mind, man!"

But it was too late; I was already in motion.

When I stepped into the corridor, I stumbled upon something resembling a scene out of a movie. It was complete chaos: windows were being broken; fires were being set; here and there, inmates were carrying TVs and radios, darting through wafts of smoke. Seeing this, I rushed to my cell to secure my personal belongings.

"Meet me back here!" I called out to my workout partner, who immediately struck off down the corridor toward his pod.

I was housed in L-6, the pod where most of the killings allegedly took place. Prosecutors would later use my brief sojourn back to the pod as "proof" that I participated in the murders. However, they would neglect to mention to the jury that I had been assigned to L-6 and had every right to be there.

When I walked into the pod, the first thing I noticed were guards, handcuffed behind their backs, being pushed into the lower shower stalls. I also saw several inmates being shoved into unoccupied cells. It was later said that these particular inmates had been singled out as being "snitches."

Still somewhat stunned and lacking the presence of mind to act rationally, I ran down to my cell to check on my things and discovered that it, too, was being used to hold a hostage.

"What the fuck you doin' in here!" I demanded, still not fully appreciating the seriousness of the situation. Before the person in my cell could respond, I ran up to the control panel at the front of the pod and frantically tried to operate the buttons. I had only one thought in mind: *I gotta get this mothafucka outta my cell!*

Seized by a rush of adrenalin and working feverishly to activate the right button, I inadvertently opened several of the adjoining cells that were being used to hold snitches.

"What the hell you doin'!" a masked inmate yelled from the second tier, running in my direction. Before he could reach me, someone grabbed me from behind and pulled me away from the panel.

"I gotta get my stuff! I gotta get my stuff!" I protested, struggling to free myself. I was dragged out of the pod against my will and someone whom I took to be one of the leaders spoke to me. With a slow, no-nonsense tone, this person made me understand the seriousness of what was going on. And then he gave me a choice: "You can stay in here with us, or you can leave."

I chose to leave.

I was back on the yard by approximately 3:30 p.m., a fact that was corroborated by a number of witnesses who testified at my trial. This means that somewhere between 30 and 45 minutes had elapsed since the guard first came running out of the building and the time I made my way back onto the yard. Furthermore, I was only inside the building for 10 or so minutes. In this short span of time, the prosecutors claimed I organized a "death squad" and presided over the deaths of four suspected snitches.

Not only was this an improbable accusation, it was an outright lie. After all, how could I—with no prior calculations or gang affiliations—enter into an organized demonstration and go on such a murderous rampage? It did not happen.

When the Ohio State Highway Patrol and National Guard showed up on the scene, I was not alone in assuming that it would only be a matter of time before order was restored. How that would occur, none of us knew. Some of the old heads began evoking the memory of Attica, referring to the 1971 prison uprising in New York where prisoners took over, and armed forces of the State stormed the prison, killing 29 prisoners and 10 guards. Listening to them talk, I thought about my friends who had stayed behind and were now trapped inside. I did not want them to be killed.

As the minutes ticked away, a heavily-armed S.W.A.T. team in full riot gear took up position around the perimeter fence, painting an ominous picture. Soon, helicopters were flying overhead, hovering in midair as though about to fire rockets at the prison. Taking it all in, I roamed the yard in a state of bewilderment, watching, listening, waiting. After about three hours or so, as the sun began to set, I got a bit anxious. *It'll be getting dark soon,* I thought, wondering how long it would be before the State made its move. *Are we gonna be out here all night? What are they waiting on?*

And then, as if out of a dream, a masked inmate emerged from inside the building brandishing what appeared to be a machete. And following immediately behind him were two masked inmates carrying what appeared to be a body. I was sitting on the boxing ring about 50 yards away and it was kind of hard to see what was going on through the mass of people who had congregated near the L-side entrance.

"That's a dead body!" someone exclaimed. And then an audible murmur went up as the realization set in.

Hell, naw! I said to myself, getting up and making my way toward the building. I wanted to see if it was one of my friends. When I finally made my way through the throng of people, I was relieved to discover that it was not anyone I knew. Still, it was a stunning development. If anyone had doubts about whether or not the authorities would storm the building, those doubts could now be put to rest. Surely the State would not sit back and watch more dead bodies be dumped on the yard. Would they?

But sit back and watch they did. After the first body was brought out and subsequently retrieved, a strange and somber cycle ensued. A body was dumped, a crowd gathered to see who it was—hoping against hope that it was not someone they knew—and then the Patrol came out with their weapons drawn and recovered the corpse. It was an agonizing experience, standing there waiting to see who the next body would be. Meanwhile, the people whose job it was to intervene did nothing. Apparently, they had been given the order to stand down. But why? How many more people needed to die?

As I stood there, it occurred to me that one of the dead bodies could have easily been mine. Indeed, any one of us could still be killed right there on the spot, right in front of the police, and they would have done nothing to stop it. It was complete anarchy.

Night had now come upon the scene, and people began

separating themselves into protective clusters: blacks on one side, whites on the other. No one made an open declaration, but it was obvious that fear was setting in. Brief but violent skirmishes over territory broke out as knives and lines were drawn. When the temperature dropped, bonfires made out of the wood stripped from the boxing ring sprung up in haphazard heaps all over the yard. It tore my heart out to see the ring being dismantled; it had served as the place of my redemption, the place where I had exorcised my demons and reclaimed my sense of purpose and worth. And now it, too, was being killed—ripped apart and burned right before my eyes.

Who could have imagined, at the beginning of what started out as an ordinary day, that things would end in such madness? And it was not over yet. At around 2 o'clock in the morning, after we had already lived through a certain kind of hell, the Ohio State Highway Patrol finally came out onto the yard and "rescued" us. With automatic weapons pointed at our heads, we were ordered to line up and march into K-block's gymnasium, where we were stripped naked and forced, with our hands now fastened behind our backs, to sit on the cold floor like animals.

After about two hours or so, we were placed in random groups of 10 and then forced into cells that were designed to accommodate one person.

I ended up in a cell with Dennis Weaver, one of the nine inmates killed during the disturbance. I could not have known it at the time, but the events surrounding Dennis' death, and my future efforts to persuade inmates not to speak with the authorities, became the basis around which the State would later charge me with multiple murders. But I am getting a little ahead of myself.

K-block gymnasium—April 12, 1993[2]

The first thing I need to make abundantly clear is that, prior to us being thrown into the cell together, Dennis and I had never officially met. I saw him around the prison on occasion; in fact, he refereed a few of the institutional football games I played in. Beyond that, he was a virtual stranger to me. Based on my limited observation, he was an "old-timer," someone who had been in prison for a very long time and who was consequently treated with a certain amount of deference. Judging by his all-gray Afro and beard, he was in his early-to-mid sixties. Medium height and slight of build, his days of striking an imposing figure were long behind him. And this, ultimately, was the reason why he was killed: he was too old and frail to protect himself.

Besides Dennis and me, the following are the names of the other eight inmates who were in the cell with us:

---

[2] Source: http://retro.cincinnati.com/Topics/Gallery/Lucasville-Prison-Riot; December 29, 2013

1. Hiawatha Frezzell
2. William "Geno" Washington
3. Ricky Rutherford
4. Michael Childers
5. William (Shabaz) Bowling
6. John Malveaux
7. Eric Scales and
8. Jeffrey Mack

When the doors slammed behind us on that fateful day, I immediately made my way to the back of the cell and pressed my back against the wall. Looking around, I was somewhat relieved to see that I was among at least a few familiar faces. Like me, Eric and Jeffrey (or "DJ," as he was called) were from Cleveland, Ohio. When our eyes met, we gave each other a nod of recognition to signal that we had each other's backs.

Out of the 10 of us, Eric was the first to find his way out of the flimsy restraints that we were in, and then, one by one, we were all set free. Still naked with little to no room to move around, it was inevitable that a skin-on-skin encounter would occur and, when it did, tempers flared. William Bowling in particular, seemed overly agitated by the circumstances. He had been fussing and cussing from the moment he stepped into the cell, railing against the police. "These mothafuckas treatin' us like animals!" he exclaimed, referring to the naked state we were in. He was at the front of the cell, holding on to the bars, screaming hysterically, "The white man is the devil! The white man is the devil!" With the noise level being so loud, I doubt if anyone could hear him.

William and I had crossed paths before. We briefly worked together in the kitchen, scrubbing pots and pans, one of the hardest and dirtiest jobs in general population. No one wanted to work in the pots-n-pans room. In fact, it was one of the assignments typically given as a form of punishment. What had I done? I was caught crossing the yellow line in the corridor one day, and the punishment for this minor indiscretion was to wash pots and pans for a month; either that, or do a 15-day stint in the hole.

I had no idea why William was there. He never told me and I never asked. As far as I could tell from his incessant rambling, he had been there for months on end and was very upset about it. Not a day went by that he did not lash out in anger over the evident injustice of his ordeal. However, something told me that if it were not the pots and pans, it would have been something else; he walked around with a perpetual scowl on his face.

After about five hours or so, white jumpsuits were thrown into the cell and we hurried to clothe ourselves. Turning away from the bars, William decided to direct his anger at Michael, the only white guy in the cell. He went on a rant about how white people were nothing more than cavemen who bore a genetic disease that made them inherently evil. "You evil, bitch!" he yelled, daring Michael to say something. Michael, refusing to take the bait, looked at William with a bland expression on his face. And then William moved on to the next person, found his point of ridicule, and dared whomever he was talking to to say something. By the time he got to me, I had heard enough and, instead of words, unleashed a three-punch combination to his face. I could tell from his shocked expression that he was not expecting that. He staggered back, wide-eyed, holding his hand to his mouth.

"What's up, nigga?" I asked, challenging him. He looked at me, thought about it, and then backed down. "That's what I thought, coward-ass mothafucka."

The one thing I cannot stand is a bully.

Presently, sandwiches were thrown into the cell, and we all scrambled to the front and staked our claim. We had not eaten in over 24 hours and the lack of food caused us to behave like animals. Dennis was the only one who had maintained his dignity; he refused to move and was knocked to the floor. When he made it back to his feet, he lashed out at William who, holding two or three sandwiches, had obviously taken more than his share.

"You call yourself a Muslim, talking all that shit about the white man—why you ain't stay inside [L-block] with the rest of the Muslims?" Dennis wanted to know. He had a good point.

"Yeah, why you ain't stay yo' coward-ass inside?" Eric asked, adding fuel to the fire.

I stood back and watched. It was kind of amusing to see William grope in the darkness of his mind for a quick comeback. He could have easily told them that the reason he didn't stay inside was because he was a member of the Nation of Islam, and not affiliated with the Sunni Muslims who had taken over L-side. However, unable to think logically, he turned his attention back to Dennis and the two began arguing again. Dennis, picking up on Eric's swipe, called William a coward. William countered by calling Dennis a fag and a snitch. After a brief exchange of blows, the two began to tussle, and Dennis ended up in a headlock. Before long, he began gasping for air and struggling wildly to free himself.

"Grab his legs! Grab his legs!" William screamed out to Michael and Ricky, who immediately sprang into action. Soon, and quite unexpectedly, Dennis lost consciousness and died.

When the odor from his evacuated bowels filled the cell, we all called out for the guard and, after about 30 minutes or so, they came and removed Dennis' body. Gruesome stuff.

Later, when I was on trial for my life, the prosecutor—inquiring about Dennis' death—asked, "Why didn't you try to stop it?"

"It wasn't my responsibility," I said, feeling defensive.

In hindsight, I realize that this was a callous thing to say. However, be that as it may, I did not kill Dennis. I did not put him in that cell. I did not wrap my arms around his neck to deprive him of air or hold him down when he could not breathe. And contrary to what the State alleged, I did not give the order for Dennis to be killed. Yes, I should have tried to intervene; after all, that would have been the human thing to do. But the truth of the matter is that at that particular point in my young life I was not in touch enough with my humanity to understand the implications of my callousness. So call me heartless, if you must. However, the first rule of doing time is "mind your own business," which is exactly what I did.

In early questioning regarding Dennis' death, I lied and told investigators that I was asleep when Dennis was killed. Though untrue, it was my way of saying, "I don't want to get involved." And I was not the only one who kept quiet; we all did. That is, everyone except William. He admitted from the start that he was responsible for Dennis' death, although his admission came with the convenient caveat: "*They* made me do it."

William claimed that Eric and I forced him to kill Dennis.[3] It was his bruised ego that prompted him to say this. In a heated moment of agitation he had confronted me and, with a few well-placed blows, I exposed him for the coward that he actually was—and now he was trying to take me down with him.

Later, after I was assigned the role of death-squad leader, William's lie became something of a catchphrase when—after the State assembled their team of informants—perpetrator after perpetrator claimed I forced them to kill.

---

[3] Eric was never charged with Dennis' death.

"He made me do it," they said. And yet, it has never been sufficiently explained how I forced all these inmates to kill, or why I went on such a murderous crusade to cleanse the prison of all its snitches.

According to the record, this is what the State maintained:

> LaMar, who was not a Muslim, did not plan or participate in the prison takeover and was in the prison recreation yard when the riot began. But after the commotion began, LaMar and two other inmates, Louis Jones and Derek Cannon, went back inside L-block to check the personal belongings in their respective cells. When the three were unable to get back outside because the Muslims had closed access to and from L-block, LaMar said to Jones and Cannon, "Ain't no need in us staying in here getting caught up in something we're not a part of. Let's kill all the snitches and get out to the yard."[4]

So, if the State is to be believed, I killed because I was trapped inside and *did not* want to be involved in the uprising. Thus, in order to not be involved, I did the very thing that would immerse me in the madness. And then, when I finally made it outside and was apparently free from the danger that I went to such great lengths to escape, I allegedly killed again, immersing myself even further. Does this make sense?

To a jury in Ironton, Ohio, it did. They listened as the State rolled out one improbable scenario after another and then found me guilty and sentenced me to death. But the

---

[4] *State v. Lamar*, 95 Ohio St.3d 181 (Ohio 2002). For full document, see www.keithlamar.org.

point in restating these things is not to cast aspersions or vent my animosity over what was done. After all, those recriminations, that anger, hurled into the past, would be a waste of time. My aim is merely to present the facts and let you, the public, decide whether or not I deserve to die. Since it will be in your name that my murder—should it occur—will be carried out, you should know the truth. And my hope is that the truth will set you free to demand that justice be done. Please keep reading...

Investigation:
A Search for Informants

When we were taken from the cell where Dennis was killed, seven of us—Eric, Michael, Ricky, Hiawatha, DJ, Geno, and I— were placed into a strip cell (i.e. a cell that has been stripped of its toilet, sink, and bed). Here, in a space no larger than a closet, we were forced to eat, sleep, and suffer for eight long, agonizing days. With no running water, there was no way for us to brush our teeth or bathe. In place of regular meals, we were given peanut butter sandwiches that were smashed and then shoved under the two-inch opening at the bottom of the cell door which, being the only source of ventilation, was instantly re-sealed in order to sustain the sauna-like conditions that we were being subjected to.

Naturally, there came a time when one of us had to use the toilet—a hole cut into the center of the floor—which could only be flushed by one of the guards who was stationed on the outside of the door, but who, out of sheer perversity, routinely refused to push the button. In a room with no air, each of us pouring down in sweat, we had to sit and endure the smell of our accumulated shit. As one might predict, it was under these and similar conditions that some—including Michael and Ricky—decided to join the rapidly growing team of informants.

With no physical evidence linking anyone to crimes, the State began its fact-finding mission by making it clear that they were not interested in facts. Instead of trying to find out what really happened, they would create a story and hire actors to read the lines (or "lies," I should say)—and there was no shortage of individuals who were willing to sell their souls in order to escape the hellish conditions that we were being put through. After a few torturous months, the team was assembled and moved to Oakwood Correctional Facility in Lima, Ohio, where a whole wing had been set aside to accommodate our weak-willed brethren. This is where they went over the script, the place where all the lies were rehearsed and refined in preparation for trial.

Prosecutors would later deny that these informants received any "special treatment"; after all, that would have been unethical. Yet, rampant rumors of catered meals and free commissary sounded around the clock. Were the rumors true? There was no way to know at the time, but what was done in the dark would eventually come to light.

While preparing for a 2007 evidentiary hearing, my attorneys conducted a taped deposition of an inmate informant named Anthony Walker who was housed at Oakwood during the time in question. He confirmed that staff "catered to our every whim." According to him, they had access to unlimited supplies from the canteen, such as cigarettes, food, candy and so on. They even received food and clothes boxes from home and had the run of the pod to which they were assigned.

Another inmate informant, Emanuel "Buddy" Newell, described a separate event at Oakwood in a signed affidavit wherein he detailed how their "handlers" (including Special Prosecutor Mark Piepmeier) celebrated with them:

Our handlers arranged a Thanksgiving dinner festival, which our handlers personally attended, exclusively for those of us in the witness protection program in the special housing block. The Thanksgiving dinner consisted of pies, popcorn, cakes, doughnuts, candy and so forth. The message was that our handlers and we were part of one single family unit and that we were to reciprocate the allegiance and loyalty that they were exhibiting toward us. We were often referred to as "the Piepmeier family."

Did Mr. Piepmeier really think of these opportunists as *family*? Probably not. But he was staking his reputation on them, individuals whom he knew were willing to lie in order to save themselves. What else could he have done to ensure their allegiance? True, he could have acknowledged that, without any physical evidence, it was impossible to know with certainty who had done what; but then again, had he done that, the State would have more than likely hired someone else to do the job. Besides, there was a lot of money to be made, promotions to be had, and only a conscientious fool would have taken the time to consider the righteous rhetoric intoned by the criminal justice standards which state: a prosecutor's job is not to win guilty verdicts, but to see that justice is done.[5] And so Mr. Piepmeier went forward.

To create an atmosphere conducive to sharing, Piepmeier implemented an open-door policy at Oakwood that made it permissible for informants to go back and forth between cells. Indeed, they were encouraged to confer with each other, to share and exchange notes, and to help one another iron out any discrepancies that existed. As the first trials drew near, boardroom style meetings were held wherein informants sat around a table and received last-minute instructions from prosecutors. Years later, as the details of these goings-on were made known, Oakwood was rightfully dubbed, "The Snitch Academy."

Still, though much has been made known since that

---

[5] http://www.americanbar.org/publications/criminal_justice_section_archive/crimjust_standards_pfunc_blkold.html, January 11, 2014

time, it remains unclear how and when I became the leader of the so-called death squad. What I believe happened is this:

A man by the name of Anthony Lavelle, who was the professed leader of the Black Gangster Disciples—one of the gangs thought by many to be responsible for most of the killings during the uprising, including, most significantly, the death of the guard—became the State's star witness. His testimony was needed to secure guilty verdicts against the leaders of the Sunni Muslims and Aryan Brotherhood. Hence, in order to give him a veneer of "believability," I believe the State removed him from the role of death-squad leader and shifted that role onto me, someone who was serving a life sentence and apparently had nothing to lose. They assumed I would buckle under and take a deal, which would have allowed them to clear their books and put a period behind the whole messy ordeal. And they did this knowing full well that I was innocent.

In fact, on June 23, 1994, more than a year after the uprising, a member of the Black Gangster Disciples named Aaron Jefferson came forward and admitted to killing an inmate named Darrell Depina, someone whom I would later be convicted of murdering. Indeed, Aaron admitted to murdering two inmates: Darrell Depina and David Sommers. He also admitted to assaulting Emanuel "Buddy" Newell, the informant who described the Thanksgiving feast that Special Prosecutor Mark Piepmeier attended.

Aaron was eventually charged and convicted for Sommers' murder. However, when it came to the death of Depina, it was conveniently decided that his admissions were "unreliable." Yet, a brief reading of the interview clearly demonstrates that the opposite was the case: it was about the death of Sommers, not Depina, that the interviewer expressed doubts. After Aaron alleged to have struck

Sommers "eight or nine times with a baseball bat," the following exchange ensued:

Q: Well, Aaron let me explain one thing to you.

A: Yeah.

Q: I know about Sommers' case.

A: Uh, huh.

Q: And Sommers wasn't hit 8-9 times in the head. Okay. And you're telling me he was. Now we're not going to sit in here and take a -- any type of statement from you and like I explained to you before, if you're going to tell me something you tell me something that you know to be fact and not something that you heard...

And then later:

Q: If you're going to sit here, I want you to tell me the truth.

A: I'm telling you...

Q: I don't want you to exaggerate anything.

A: I'm not exager---I mean...

Q: Cause if you exaggerate one thing, then I don't know what else you'd exaggerate on, especially something I know to be fact -- that I know you're lying about.

Clearly, based on the above exchange, the interviewer had serious misgivings about Aaron's story and whether or not he had anything to do with Sommers' death. Further on, in the same interview, Aaron began to describe the assault on Emanuel "Buddy" Newell and, once again, the interviewer questioned his credibility:

A: So I just went to L-6 cell 36 and, uh, was playing it like, you know, letting him know that he was to walk out with me out to the yard because everybody else was gone, man. So, you know what I'm saying? You don't want to be left behind here, you don't want them guys [State Highway Patrol] coming -- you know them folks come running up in on you. Come with me, take you into the yard.

Q: Now you told Buddy this?

A: I tell Buddy this.

Q: Were you by yourself?

A: Yeah.

Q: Now, were you?

A: Yeah, yeah, I was...

Q: I don't think you're telling me the truth now?

It must have seemed strange that someone would willingly admit to committing such serious crimes. There had to be some kind of angle, some other reason besides his conscience that was driving him to do this. When asked what he wanted for his confession, Aaron responded:

> A: That, the guys that's being accused that didn't do this be let go. Be left alone. That's the only thing that I want in exchange for. It might not seem like a hell of a lot. It might not seem much to you or to anybody else. It means a lot to me though.

> Q: Aaron, let me tell you something. You're going to sit here and admit to me that you were involved in murders...

> A: Yeah.

> Q: ...and we have evidence to prove that what you're telling me is not true. How would we ever convict you of that?

It was an excellent question, but convict him they did. They gave poor Aaron a life sentence for coming forward and admitting his guilt. And then, on July 29, 1994, a month after Aaron's confession, they charged me with Depina's death and the deaths of four other inmates: Dennis Weaver, Bruce Vitale, Albert Staiano, and Wiliam Svette (Author's note: unbeknownst to me at the time, an inmate named Frederick Frakes had already been indicted for the death of William Svette on May 19, 1994, two months before I was indicted for the very same crime. However, after I was pegged as the leader of the death squad, his indictment mysteriously disappeared).

This is a mistake, I thought, frantically searching the indictment for my name. Finding it, I went deeper into denial. *This can't be right,* I told myself. *Nine (9) counts of aggravated murder, with death-penalty specifications!*

Unable to think straight, I asked my neighbor to look the document over for me. "They sayin' I killed nine people, man," I told him, passing the indictment through the bars.

The whole pod grew quiet, eavesdropping as my neighbor tried to put things in perspective for me.

"Yeah, yeah, yeah," he finally said after he was done reading it. He cleared his throat. "They're charging you with nine counts, not nine bodies," he clarified, "and the specifications mean you're eligible for the death penalty. They're going to try to put you on death row, Keith!" he announced.

I heard the alarm in his voice.

"Get the fuck out of here!" I said, more out of disbelief than defiance. I was stunned. *Put me on death row for what?*

For weeks I staggered around in a state of shock, unable to comprehend my thoughts and feelings. *What is going on? How did this happen?*

Before April 11, 1993, I had never been particularly outspoken or interested in becoming a radical (whatever that means?). However, standing there as dead bodies were dumped onto the yard (while those in authority stood back and did nothing), and then experiencing the shock of witnessing Dennis' death, awakened something in me.

"Fuck the police!" became my attitude when it came to helping the State with their investigation. As far as I was concerned, they had literally left us for dead—and now they wanted us to become informants? *Fuck that!* Given what we had gone through, a great many of us felt the same way. And being placed under "investigation" only added insult to injury.

"When is this madness gonna end?" many of us wondered aloud. "How much more of this shit are we gonna have to take?"

Soon, in response to our mounting anger and frustration,

we started trashing the range with food and garbage after agreeing among ourselves that none of us would come out to clean it up.

"Let the police do it!"

And for a few days, they did. They swept and mopped and carried mounds of garbage out of the pod as we all taunted them: "Clean it up, bitches!"

And then some of the old heads started holding forth about the virtues of solidarity and sticking together against the administration:

"They need us. We don't need them. Keep your mouth shut and we can change the whole prison system."

Every night there was a variation of this same speech, and I listened to it over and over again until something took root in me. I became openly critical of the mistreatment we had all undergone and, for a few months at least, was serious in my determination to persuade others not to join the administration in their efforts to further divide and conquer us.

Yeah, it's us against them, I told myself. Before long, I was speaking out against becoming an informant, sharing the horrifying details of my recent experiences. Just the thought of someone stepping across the line to help "them" was the ultimate betrayal, especially after all we had been forced to endure.

One day, after we had trashed the range again, the guards brought an inmate porter in to clean it up, and some of the old heads pulled him to the side and explained what we had going on.

"This is a demonstration, young blood, and we don't want you over here doing their dirty work. Let them do it...."

But the young blood did not listen. He came back day after day until, one day, an old head lured him up to the bars of his cell and stuck a knife in his neck. He got the message after that.

While all of this was going on, I was cultivating a more political perception of things by reading, studying, and learning about power dynamics through the lens of people such as Huey P. Newton, Elaine Brown, George Jackson, Angela Davis, and Assata Shakur.

It was Assata Shakur and George Jackson that had the greatest impact on my mentality, though. Assata (aka JoAnne Chesimard) had been found guilty of trumped-up charges and, while serving her time in federal prison, managed to escape to Cuba. Her indomitable spirit and sense of determination in the face of seemingly insurmountable odds inspired me. It was because of her that I would ultimately change my name, adopting the African attributes Bomani Hondo Shakur to serve as a constant reminder of how I should carry myself. Taken together, my new name translated into Mighty Soldier/Prepared for War/the Thankful.

As for George Jackson, it was inevitable that I would respond to him. Like me, he had come to prison when he was still a young man and, after being exposed to the raw racism that prevailed therein, had undergone a radicalization of his thought processes—and now I was undergoing a similar transformation. I poured over his book, *Soledad Brother*, with awe and admiration. I was amazed that someone could think and feel so deeply about life. Reading through the letters he had written to his family and friends gave me a definite sense of urgency and purpose. *This is what it means to be alive*, I thought, as I read his words of defiance.

Stand up and be heard! Never allow yourself to be counted among the broken ones!

I took him seriously. I stood up. I spoke out. I made myself a target.

Trial: Mockery of Justice

And still more often, the condemned is the
burden-bearer for the guiltless and unblamed.
—Kahlil Gibran[6]

Since I was already serving 18 years-to-life, charging me with nine counts of aggravated murder was more bluff than blunder. The State never expected me to go forward and demand a trial. Why would I? Even if by some miracle I prevailed, they could still keep me in prison for the rest of my life. So they offered me a deal: "Cop out to murder and the time will run concurrent with the time you're already doing."

"Why are y'all doin' this?" I asked, genuinely bewildered. "Y'all know I didn't kill those people. I wasn't even in there!" I exclaimed, growing angrier by the minute.

"C'mon on, Keith," they said, using my first name as if we were old friends, "we didn't come here to talk to you about whether or not you did it. We're here to offer you a deal; and it's a very good one, by the way. With good behavior, you could be out by the time you're in your early fifties."

It angered and amazed me that they could calculate so easily the years of my life, as if three decades were nothing. Still, I would be lying if I said I did not consider it. I mean, I understood the position I was in. Indeed, I understood it all too well: in one form or another, I had been dealing with the criminal justice system since I was 13 years old. However, in each of the prior convictions against me—one as a juvenile and two as an adult—I was guilty of the crimes for which I was charged and, therefore, willingly threw myself on the mercy of the court. Believe me, I knew what a deal was and

---

6 Kahlil Gibran, "On Crime and Punishment," *The Prophet* (Alfred A. Knopf, 1923).

if, as the State alleged, I was guilty of taking the lives of five people, I would have once again thrown myself on the mercy of the court. But I did not do this, and a deal is not a deal when you are being asked to forfeit the rest of your life for something you did not do.

"No!" I said no and went forward under the illusion that justice was real and that *the truth*, as the saying goes, *would set me free*. Was I being naïve? Yes, yes—the answer is yes. Like most people who are a product of the public school system, I, too, pledged allegiance to the flag and sang "My Country 'Tis of Thee"—and even though I chose a life of lawlessness, these ideals nevertheless burrowed their way into my psyche and convicted me even when I thought I had gotten away with my crimes.

I went to trial because I believed in the system, in the process of justice. However, I was on my way to finding out that the truth can only set you free when you have enough money to level the playing field.

When you are poor in this country and are unable to pay for your own legal representation, the State is obligated to see that you are provided with competent counsel. And if you have the added misfortune, as I did, of being charged with a capital offense, that obligation immediately doubles and you are provided with two attorneys, all to ensure that you are equally and properly protected under the law (as stated in the Fourteenth Amendment to the Constitution).

And, yes, it all sounds very good on paper. However, in reality, there exist two separate systems: one for those who have money and a very different one for the poor. Innocent or not, trials cost money, and the system—notwithstanding the high and mighty talk of the Constitution—is not designed to dole out freebies. Yes, if you are indigent, you will be provided with two capital attorneys, but they won't be equally and properly compensated; consequently, in most cases, they won't be sufficiently prepared or motivated to mount the kind of defense that a death-penalty case requires.

In the present instance, State attorneys were paid $100 an hour in addition to the sums they were making in their home counties, while defense attorneys were only paid $30 an hour for out-of-court time and $40 an hour for time spent inside the courtroom. And since there was no interim billing, defense attorneys were forced to wait until the termination of each individual case before they were paid. From the very beginning, then, a climate was created to induce defense attorneys to persuade their clients to cop out, which is exactly what happened in the majority of cases.

I got lucky when Herman Carson and K. Robert Toy (two attorneys out of Athens, Ohio) were appointed to represent me. When I was first indicted, the State assigned another attorney to my case. I forget his name, but it was apparent that he was there to deliver a message: "They're going to try to kill you, Keith," he told me on our very first visit. I immediately complained and he was replaced with Herman and Robert.

However, this does not mean that I automatically trusted them. After meeting them for the first time, I was put off by Herman's "good old boy" handlebar mustache. *He's a redneck*, was my first impression, but to my relief and surprise we were able to build the necessary client/attorney relationship. In fact, Herman went above and beyond the call of duty. He provided me with all the necessary legal books and information I needed to educate myself about the process I was about to undergo. And then, on the eve of trial, he pleaded with me to not proceed.

"The deck is stacked against you, Keith," he told me, with a sad expression on his face.

"I know, Herman," I replied, wishing I could somehow explain to him why I could not accept the State's deal.

Aside from being innocent, I had been copping out my whole life, it seemed, and I was tired of it. I copped out on my childhood by growing up too fast; I copped out on my friends and family by becoming a criminal; I copped out on my education by dropping out of school; I copped out on my community by selling drugs to my neighbors; and, as a last and final insult to myself, I had taken someone's life, the ultimate cop out.

If the State had decided that I deserved to die when I was initially convicted for murder in 1989, I would not have argued the point. After all, I felt and believed all along that taking someone's life was unforgivable. However, by the grace of whatever gods may be, my life was spared and I took that as a sign that it was time to do something productive with my potential. This is why I earned my GED and enrolled in the college program—I was trying to turn my life around. Thus, when I was presented with the proposition to cop out yet again (but this time for something I did *not* do), I could not bring myself to do it.

Originally, my case was set to be tried in Portsmouth, Ohio, a small town just up the road from SOCF. However, because of the uproar surrounding the death of the guard and the prejudicial climate it created, I was granted a change of venue and my trial was promptly moved to Ironton, Ohio, a virtually all-white city less than 40 miles away from the prison.

Instead of moving my trial to a more racially diverse city like Dayton, Cleveland, or Columbus, where jury pools were more likely to include people of my own race, my trial was intentionally kept in a city where 93.3% of its inhabitants were white. Now, I do not mean to suggest that race is the only factor that contributes to the outcome of a criminal case; however, it would be disingenuous to pretend that it does not figure significantly into things. Let us be real: despite all the talk to the contrary, we do not live in a post-racial society (then or now), and my case was moved to Ironton to further stack the deck against me. Even the judge, the Honorable Fred W. Crow, III, was handpicked from neighboring Meigs County, where the only thing black is the pavement on its streets.

So, yes, I could see the storm clouds gathering, so to speak, but that did not deter me. I still wanted my day in court. I still wanted a jury to listen to the evidence and find me *not guilty* of these lies.

Speaking of evidence, we had only received the bare minimum at this point and almost nothing in the way of "exculpatory" material—that is, *evidence favorable to the defense*. In October, 1994, my attorneys filed a motion to compel exculpatory evidence, and the judge called us to a March 6, 1995, pre-trial hearing to hear our arguments.

It was at this hearing that the State first hinted at its strategy. When my attorneys argued in defense of our motion, the prosecutors vehemently resisted the idea of turning over favorable evidence. According to them, all statements were given with the State's promise of confidentiality. Surprisingly, Judge Crow allowed them to proffer this flimsy excuse as a justifiable reason why they could not produce the requested evidence. My attorneys strenuously objected to such an erroneous excuse.

As a compromise, the State reluctantly agreed to turn over the names of 43 inmates who had been interviewed by the Ohio State Highway Patrol. Shockingly, the names were given without the corresponding statements that had been made. Instead, an 11-page document containing very brief summaries was handed over to the judge, and he, in complete collusion with the State, read aloud snippets of what was said:

1. He identified inmate Abraham D. as a person that assaulted Depina and possibly killed him with a baseball bat or a stick and identified Charles O., Rasheem M., and James R. as being involved in the assault or killing of Depina.

2. He said that inmate Stanford H. was an ex-lover of Vitale who said he would get him after they broke up.

3. He implicated Frederick F. in the Vitale homicide.

4. He identified Thomas Taylor as beating Staiano to death with a baseball bat.

5. He identified inmate Sterling B. as striking Svette with a mop ringer; inmate Sean D. as striking Svette with a curl bar; and Leroy E. as striking Svette with a stick; inmate Willie J. as involved in the homicide.

6. He indicated that Frederick F. was responsible for Svette's homicide on L corridor ramp.

7. He observed inmate Stacey Gordon strike Svette in the head with a bat.

8. He stated he observed inmate Brian E. kill Svette in L-corridor.

9. He denied speaking to LaMar about the Weaver homicide. He stated that LaMar was not responsible for Weaver's death but he would not identify any suspects.

On and on it went until finally my attorney, Mr. Toy, had heard enough:

Mr. Toy: Your Honor, may I address something for the record?

Judge Crow: You may.

Mr. Toy: Thank you very much, your Honor.

Your Honor, with the Court reading this information with these names, my quick calculation comes to -- I would estimate 20 or more new names that I have not heard of before. We have less than three weeks till we begin a trial. These are people that -- names that I have not heard of at all in this particular matter; and we need, obviously, time to get this information.

In keeping with his strange rulings, Judge Crow failed to force the prosecution to turn over the complete statements. Instead, he suggested we embark on a wild goose chase and flippantly offered my attorneys more time and additional funds to hire an investigator to interview each of the potential witnesses as a way to ascertain who had said what. As expected, my attorneys, no doubt thinking about the lack of interim billing and the time it would take to complete the task, respectfully declined the offer and turned their attention toward voir dire: the selection of the jury.

Out of the 100 or so people who showed up for jury duty in my trial, only two were African Americans. Not surprisingly, the State (with the help of Judge Crow) immediately set about removing them from the pool.

In a capital case, both sides are allowed six peremptory

challenges, which means each side can remove a prospective juror without showing just cause. For example, if the prosecutor does not like the color of someone's shirt, he can ask that that person be removed, no explanation required. However, before the prosecutor is forced to squander one of his very valuable challenges, he first attempts to have the unfavorable candidate removed by proving just cause. Say, for instance, a prospective juror does not believe in the imposition of the death penalty, s/he will not be allowed to sit on the jury. If it can be proven that someone is a racist, s/he will be asked to leave, so on and so forth.

As it so happened, an African-American lady in her mid-sixties named Tabitha, was deeply religious. To disqualify her from serving on my jury, the prosecutor questioned her interpretation of the commandment "Thou Shalt Not Kill" as a way to determine whether or not she believed in the imposition of the death penalty. It was a shameless—and shameful—trap. But poor old Tabitha proved smarter than expected and stayed clear of being automatically excused. Finally, when it was obvious that she was not going to take the bait, the prosecutor used one of his peremptory challenges and had her removed. And then he used another challenge to remove the last remaining African American.

I did not know it at the time, but removing the only two African Americans from the jury pool was against the law, as delineated in *Batson v. Kentucky*, 476 US 79, which says that "the Equal Protection Clause forbids the prosecutor to challenge potential jurors solely on account of their race or on the assumption that black jurors as a group will be unable to impartially consider the State's case against a black defendant."

These are nice sounding words. However, as with all things dealing with the criminal justice system, rules are followed and/or broken based on how much power one has to compel adherence. In other words, the strong (rich) do what they have the power (money) to do, and the weak (poor) accept what they have to accept (injustice). This is how the system works and is the reason why so many poor people are behind bars. But I digress.

As intended, I ended up with an all-white jury. After both sides gave their opening statements, the State called eight witnesses to the stand:

1. Thomas Taylor took the stand and said I forced him to kill Albert Staiano. He described in graphic detail how he, while allegedly following my orders, bashed Albert's head in with a fire extinguisher. The jury looked at me and glared.

2. Stacey Gordon took the stand and said I was the leader of the death squad. He admitted that he never saw me "swing or strike anyone."

3. Anthony Walker took the stand and said I was the leader of the death squad. He claimed to have been standing at the back of the pod at the time that the killings were taking place.

4. Bobby Bass took the stand and said he saw me enter L-6 sometime at the beginning of the uprising. According to him, I had a mask on, but he claimed to still have been able to recognize me. He admitted he didn't actually see me harm or assault anyone.

5. Louis Jones took the stand and said he was in the death squad along with me. He is the one who put forth the story that, in order to get back on the yard, we brokered a deal with the Muslims to kill snitches in L-6.

6. Ricky Rutherford took the stand and said I forced him to kill Dennis Weaver.

7. Michael Childers took the stand and said I forced him to kill Dennis Weaver.

8. John Malveaux took the stand and said I forced William Bowling to kill Dennis Weaver.

Surprisingly, William refused to take the stand. In fact, on the morning he was due to testify against me, we had a chance encounter that possibly gave him a change of heart. I saw him sitting in the prison transport van outside the courthouse as I made my way to the side entrance of the building. I was being escorted by a group of heavily armed deputies and, when they paused to unlock the door, I turned and looked directly into his eyes. By then, it had been two years since we had last seen each other. I shook my head in disgust. "You wrong, man," I said, before I was hurried off.

Did this brief encounter awaken his conscience? Possibly. Like most of the State's witnesses, he had signed a plea agreement and, by not testifying, was exposing himself to definite penalties. I was impressed. Still, as gratifying as the moment was, the damage had already been done.

Since the State refused to follow the law and turn over statements that would have allowed me to refute their claims, the jury never knew about the many inmates whose statements were withheld. Had I been given access to these statements during my trial, when it mattered, I could have challenged the State's case against me. Below are some of the things that I have been able to uncover since that time:

1. **Thomas Taylor:** In one of his initial interviews (#871, taken July 20, 1993) he told the State Highway Patrol that Stacey Gordon had "come down the range" with the rest of the death squad. He stated that Gordon was not wearing a mask and that [Gordon] "helped kill Vitale and Depina." Taylor later said that Gordon was in L-6 on the morning of April 15 when Officer Vallandingham was killed and, in fact, was one of two men who went to the cell on the upper range where Vallandingham was being held, and brought him down to the shower where he was murdered.

Question: What would the jury have thought if they had been privy to this information? Taylor testified that he witnessed me commit various crimes; however, at no point in his testimony did he admit to seeing Stacey Gordon, a key witness for the prosecution, participate in the murders of Vitale and Depina, as his withheld statement alleged. Was Taylor lying or telling the truth? If he was telling the truth during his initial interview, why was Gordon never charged? If he was lying, why was he testifying against me?

2. **Stacey Gordon:** The first thing that needs to be said about Gordon is that he is a supreme opportunist. According to all accounts, including his own, he was a "shot caller" during the uprising, and may have even been the leader of the death squad. Had I had Thomas Taylor's statement, I could have called him to the stand and questioned him at length about Gordon's involvement in the very murders for which Gordon had been called to testify against me. Gordon received an early parole for his testimony.

3. Anthony Walker: An inmate named Samuel Batson claimed that Anthony Walker killed Albert Staiano, one of the inmates I was convicted of killing. Had the State turned over this statement, I could have used it to show that Walker had blood on his hands and was testifying to save himself.

4. Bobby Bass: Based on his own admission, he never saw me do anything. Indeed, he only mentioned my name after it was brought up by a state trooper. He, too, was paid for his testimony with an early parole.

5. Louis Jones: He and I were never together during the uprising. He saw an opportunity to go home early and took it, plain and simple. With the help of the State, he lied about the fact that he had been given immunity. He went home five years before his release date.

6. Ricky Rutherford: Based on medical records that have been uncovered since the uprising, Ricky Rutherford suffered from auditory and visual hallucinations including, apparently, command hallucinations to kill himself. In addition, he suffered from command hallucinations to act out against others. The State should have turned over this information. We should have been made aware that Rutherford sometimes heard voices that told him to hurt people.

7. Michael Childers: According to medical records recovered since the uprising, Michael Childers was "severely mentally ill" and "believed he had a transmitter placed in his head, probably by the FBI."

8. John Malveaux: Prior to our being placed in the cell where Dennis Weaver was killed, I had never seen or spoken to John. It is very likely that he just got on the bandwagon and took advantage of the opportunity to go home early.

How someone like John could be enticed into testifying makes perfect sense when considering an example of how the game was played. The following is an excerpt taken from an actual statement of a Highway Patrol interview with another prisoner:

[Trooper 1]: I need to know what I can take to the prosecutors. What can you clear up for me that I can go tell the prosecutors about that we don't already know? I've got to have something...

[Trooper 2]: You know what they're going to say, though? They're going to say, "What can you tell us about Vallandingham?" They say that every single time. "What can this guy tell us about Vallandingham?"...

[Prisoner]: I have something for you. I'm ready to go home. I think you know what I'm saying.

[Trooper 1]: Are you going to give me Vallandingham?

[Prisoner]: Yep.

So you see, this is how it went when a guy was savvy enough to read between the lines and conjure up the nerve to come right out with "I'll say whatever you want me to say if you let me go home." Still, even with all the deals that were made, it was the withholding of exculpatory evidence that was the State's true masterstroke. They denied me the opportunity to refute their accusations by not turning over the voluminous amount of conflicting statements that directly and consistently contradicted their characterization of the facts. In other words, they tied my hands behind my back and put a muzzle over my mouth.

When it came time to present our own defense (if you can call it that), the only thing I could do was call people who saw me outside on the yard during the time the murders inside L-block were supposedly taking place. I also called someone who was in the cell when Dennis Weaver was killed. In all, I called a total of five witnesses:

1. **Ronald Foreman:** He testified that I was outside his cell window at approximately 3:10 and continued to show up throughout the day about every half hour or so.

2. **Christopher Williams:** He testified that he saw me on the yard at 3:10, after the riot started, sitting on a picnic bench and that he saw me several times that afternoon and evening on the yard. He mentioned that he talked to me at Foreman's cell at 3:30 for 10 minutes. He maintained that he saw me at 3:10 and again at 3:30, which covered the timeframe of the alleged murders in L-6.

3. Corey Perkins: He testified that he made it out onto the yard between 3:15 and 3:30 and saw me talking to Foreman, and that he saw me on the yard periodically until the Highway Patrol took us into custody.

4. Curt Ayers: He testified that he made it onto the yard about 10-20 minutes after the riot started and saw me talking to his cellie, an inmate by the name of George Ivory. He said there was nothing unusual about my attire or the way I comported myself.

5. William "Geno" Washington: He testified that he was in the cell when Dennis Weaver was killed. He explained that the conflict in the cell began when Shabaz (William Bowling) started an argument about sandwiches and then sucker-punched Dennis. A fight ensued and Shabaz instructed the white guy (Childers) to grab Weaver while Shabaz started to strangle him. According to him, Childers started chopping Weaver in the back of the neck. Continuing, he said he did not hear me say anything about Dennis, or hear me order anyone to kill him and added that at no point did I touch Weaver.

Out of the five witnesses that I called, I believed William "Geno" Washington was the most helpful. However, unbeknownst to my attorneys and me, Geno had given a prior statement that differed greatly from what he testified to at my trial. He initially had been used as a pawn for the State, going along with their story. But again, had the State turned over all the evidence both for and against me, I would have known about Williams' earlier conflicting statement and could have made an informed decision about calling him to testify on my behalf. More than likely, I would not have called him. Or, if called, I would have simply asked him to describe the horrible conditions that we were forced to live under and the stressful experiences that eventually prompted him to say whatever he thought they wanted to hear. As it stood, it looked as though I was trying to pull a fast one over on the jury, which, of course, put me at an even greater disadvantage.

Finally, I took the stand in my own defense, hoping against hope that I might be able to persuade at least one juror to see the absurdity in the State's case against me. A long line of witnesses had already taken the stand and claimed I had forced them to kill. Hence, I thought it of the utmost importance that I refute these claims. To do this, I tried to account for my whereabouts from the moment the guard came running out of the building until I was snatched from the cell. With the practiced prodding of my attorneys, I went over again the details of Dennis' death, repeating what the actual perpetrators had already testified to, but adding that I had nothing to do with it.

Q: "Did you order anybody to kill Weaver?"

A: "No, I didn't."

Q: "Did you take over the cell?"

A: "No, I didn't."

With respect to the murders on L-side, it was never within my ability to speak about what had occurred. I wasn't there. I had no association with the individuals who were murdered, and therefore had no idea why I was being singled out as the leader of the so-called "death squad." This being the case, the only thing I could do was deny the charges and state unequivocally for the record that I had nothing to do with the deaths.

Q: "All right. Directing your attention to L side."

A: "Okay."

Q: "You've heard the testimony here for the last about ten days?"

A: "Uh-huh."

Q: "Did you have anything to do with the death of Darrell Depina?"

A: "I don't even know Darrell Depina."

Q: "Did you have anything to do with the death of William Svette?"

A: "Absolutely not."

Q: "Did you have anything to do with the death of Bruce Vitale?"

A: "No."

Q: "Did you have anything to do with the death of Albert Staiano?"

A: "No, I didn't."

Did I think the jury would believe me? No. By then the

writing was on the wall: I was going to death row. Thus, I was not surprised when the jury came back a day later with a guilty verdict on all counts, officially placing my life in the balance. I had taken the stand in order to move forward without any regrets. I knew I was in for a long and hard fight, and I wanted to be able to fight it with my strength and dignity intact.

A penalty phase was then commenced, during which I was expected to present evidence that would somehow mitigate the severity of my alleged crimes. Since I maintained my innocence, I scoffed at such an idea and decided that I would not personally plead for my life. Nevertheless, a "mitigation specialist" was hired to sift through the wreckage of my misspent youth. There, to her great amazement, she discovered that, despite all and everything, I had remained an honor-roll student. But what did that mean?

It was subsequently suggested that I call my mother to the stand and have her describe the hand-to-mouth existence that I grew up in, a proposal that I immediately vetoed. "Ain't no way I'ma ask my mother to get up there and apologize for doing her best. Ain't no way!"

In her stead, an assortment of "professionals" took the stand and spoke about me and my life as if I was a wretched soul deserving of the deepest sympathy simply because I was born poor and black. I looked at the jury, and they weren't buying it. And then it was time for them to deliberate my fate. They had but three options:

1. 20 years-to-life
2. 30 years-to-life
3. Death penalty

If they recommended one of the life terms, the judge had

no choice but to impose that as my penalty. However, if they recommended the death penalty, the judge could overrule their recommendation and sentence me to life.

They recommended the death penalty for four of the murders and 30 years-to-life for the death of Albert Staiano, the inmate who was killed by Thomas Taylor. When the penalty phase was over, I was sent back to Lucasville to await sentencing.

There was a surprise waiting on me when I made it back to the prison that day. Throughout the entire court proceedings, I had remained among other prisoners in one of the segregation pods. However, when I was away on this particular day, the administration had taken it upon itself to move all my belongings to the "Death House," the cellblock where the now defunct electric chair was located. I was placed in a cell about 50 feet away from "Ol' Sparky," vulnerable and alone. It had been a long road I had traveled to get to where I was, and I felt utterly empty, devastated to the degree that made me wish for death. I lay down on the bed and closed my eyes, hoping that I would never wake up again.

But when tomorrow came the sun came with it, shining its rays into the darkest corners of my cell. With my eyes still closed, I could hear birds singing somewhere off in the distance; a lawn mower was buzzing, and I could smell fresh-cut grass wafting through the open windows. Then I understood something: *I'm alive.* With that realization, I opened my eyes and was instantly ashamed of myself for having entertained such disheartening thoughts. *What's wrong with you?* I asked myself. *It ain't over....*

While pacing back and forth, I remembered a poem by Rabindranath Tagore from *Fruit Gathering*, passed to me by a good friend of mine. "Make sure you memorize this, Bomani," the note had said. And I had. Now I recited it to myself:

> *Let me not pray to be sheltered from dangers but to be fearless in facing them.*
>
> *Let me not beg for the stilling of my pain but for the heart to conquer it.*
>
> *Let me not look for allies in life's battlefield but to my own strength.*
>
> *Let me not crave in anxious fear to be saved but hope for the patience to win my freedom.*
>
> *Grant me that I may not be a coward, feeling your mercy in my success alone; but let me find the grasp of your hand in my failure.*

I walked and talked to myself until I felt stable again. And then I sat down to write the first draft of what I intended to say at my upcoming sentencing hearing. Technically speaking, the judge could reject the jury's recommendation and sentence me to life; but since it had been through him that the prosecutor was able to violate my rights, I felt that it would be the height of stupidity to place my faith in him at this late date.

The first draft went into the toilet. *That's too tame.* A second and third draft found their way into the toilet as well. *Damn. Be brave,* a voice inside me said. *Speak from your heart.* Finally, a fourth and final draft poured out of me and captured exactly what I wanted to say. When I was finished with it, I committed it to memory.

Day by day I was regaining my strength, recovering my senses from the shock of my defeat, and then, on July 24,

1995—seventeen days after the jury had found me guilty—I received word that my grandmother had died. The news tore my heart out. She was somebody very special in my life, one of the few people who loved me unconditionally—and now she was gone. I felt her loss deep in my soul. *What kind of world is this?* I wondered, thinking about the mountain of pain I was buried under. Still, my grandmother would not want me to be disheartened. She would want me to stand up and fight, which was exactly what I intended to do.

When I arrived at the courthouse on the day of my sentencing hearing, I felt as though I had come to the end of something and that, going forward, I would not have to carry with me any of what I had already endured and conquered. I was certain that I was about to be sentenced to death. And yet, I felt strong, as if the fight had only just begun.

I met with my attorneys, Herman and Robert, to go over the "formalities," and they both seemed a little sad for me. I assured them that everything would be okay.

When I walked through the doors of the courtroom, I was stunned by the standing-room-only crowd who had assembled. I stood staring at a sea full of white people. *Where did they come from? How did they know?* It felt like I had been escorted back to the 1800s to witness a lynching. None of them had come to hear the evidence or to learn about the case; after all, that was unimportant. What mattered now was that someone was about to swing, pay the price, and that someone was me.

When the judge asked if I had anything to say before he pronounced his sentence, I stood up and spoke my piece:[7]

To begin with, I already know that there's nothing I

---

[7] Video clip of statement is available at www.keithlamar.org.

can say that hasn't already been said, but being that this is my life, I feel obligated to say something. Seems like everybody has something to say and everybody has an opinion on what they feel should be done with my life. Well, I want to say what I feel about my own life and whatnot.

Gathering my thoughts in preparation for my final statement

First, I want to say that I'm not unmindful of the great responsibility that you [Judge Crow] have. But I'm sure it's not your first time, and as you continue to serve, that it won't be your last time.

What has happened to me here, it doesn't exist in a vacuum, and it's real to me. And I realize this moment right here, it's only going to be lived just one time. Whatever happens after this point on, I'm going to have to live with it. Your life will go on. My life will go on, for however long that life may be.

So first of all, I want to say that, I want the record to reflect that I stand unbowed and unbroken by what has been allowed to transpire inside these walls within which I sought justice. I want the record to reflect that I have absolutely no faith in the system and no faith in the power that would permit such a miscarriage of justice to take place. And though I stand here convicted of nine counts of aggravated murder, I want the record to reflect that the only thing I'm guilty of is being innocent and that, once again, a man is being made to pay for the arrogant insensibility of a people who're so intoxicated by their myths that they don't realize that their so-called dream has turned into a nightmare.

Whether you realize it or not, I know right now [1995] in the State, in the United States, you have 1.5 million people incarcerated, 2.8 million on probation, and 671,000 people on parole. And it's frightening when you think about that and you think about this and you say, "Well, why is this man here?"

And I heard why he [the prosecutor] said I'm here. And I understand why everybody else thinks I'm here. But I'm here because I'm expendable to a society that has become so desperate to thwart the threat upon their precious status that they would stand by and watch an innocent man be killed; killed by the same system that would have us believe killing is wrong. What kind of justice is this?

Throughout the whole trial it's been said, repeatedly said by the prosecutor that every man must be held accountable for his actions. I agree with that. In 1988, I was caught stealing some jewelry out of a jewelry store, and because of my actions I pled guilty and was sentenced to two years imprisonment. In 1989, I killed a man by the name of Kenyatta Collins, and because of my actions I pled guilty and was sentenced to a term of 18 years-to-life imprisonment. In 1994, I was charged with nine counts of aggravated murder with death penalty specifications, but because of my actions, I pled not guilty and placed my life in the hands of an uncaring people.

The prosecutor said, "Every man must be held accountable." Indeed, every man except the man who hides behind the shield of an unjust system; a system that would kill a man based on the testimony of individuals who would have this court believe that they had microscopic microchips embedded in their brain[8]; a system that would kill a man in order to escape their responsibility, in order to escape the stupidity that would leave 15 correctional officers in charge of 400 violent men; men who have been stripped of their humanity and left to live like animals, unworthy of respect, unworthy of understanding, and unworthy of reason....

We sit here, and we judge people, you know, not understanding what they go through, not understanding what they underwent. And we just discard life like it's nothing.

I know this probably sounds ironic coming from me. But my world and the world that you live in, it's not the same world, at least it doesn't seem like it to me. And I could go on and on and on, you know, and I could beg you not to kill me, but my faith isn't going to

---

[8] In a note to the Ohio State Highway Patrol, Michael Childers told the authorities that the FBI embedded a microscopic microchip in his brain which was used to record the events surrounding Dennis Weaver's death.

allow me to do that....

I just want the record to reflect that my faith is in He who created me, and that I'm not governed by the manmade laws or the laws that have left me to live with death my whole life. I've been living with death my whole life.

Within the confinement of prison I found myself, and I'm not willing to sacrifice myself or belittle myself or bow to something that I don't believe in. And I don't believe in what took place in this courtroom.

Directing my comments to the prosecutors, seated on my left

The prosecutor hid evidence. He coached witnesses. He did numerous things, but "every man must be held accountable,"—except you all, right now on this day. But this ain't it, though. This ain't it.

That's all I've got to say.

Death Row I:
Walking Through Hell

Even though I walk through the valley of the shadow of death,
I will fear no evil....
—Psalms 23:4

After I spoke my piece, Judge Crow, as expected, sentenced me to death. Standing there, it felt as if I was in some kind of weird dream. In his closing comments from the bench, he repeatedly used the word "heinous" to describe the viciousness of the murders that had taken place and I nodded my head in  agreement. Yes, whoever was guilty of the crimes for which I had been sentenced to death needed to be rebuked and raked over the coals. But I was not that man and Judge Crow's words, though directed at me, did not have the desired effect. If anything, the blatant hypocrisy in what he said angered and upset me. After all, who was he to speak about murder and mayhem? Was it not murder when, instead of being impartial, he colluded with the prosecution to deprive me of a fair trial? And could not the word heinous be equally applied to the prosecutors' willful withholding of statements that could have proven my innocence? Hypocrite.

As the transport van pulled away from the courthouse, I shook my head in disbelief. I had come into the situation wearing rose-colored glasses, but I was leaving it totally disillusioned. *There is no justice in this world,* I concluded, clenching my fists in anger. I wanted to scream, but the extreme animosity I felt rendered me speechless. I was going to death row and there was nothing I could do or say about it.

When the van veered off the highway and took the now-familiar turn toward SOCF, I was actually glad to see it looming in the distance. My soul was tired and all I wanted to do was lie down and close my eyes. But, once again, I was in for a surprise. Instead of pulling up to the security gate, the guard drove around to the front entrance and stopped. I thought it a bit peculiar when he did that, but the whole day had been one weird occurrence after another.

Presently, a group of guards came out of the building. *What is this?* As I sat there, the transport guards got out of the van and opened the back doors. I had not noticed it at first, but another guard who had come out of the building was pulling a trolley with a box on it. Looking at it more closely now, I saw my name on the box. And then it hit me: *I'm leaving.* The guards had assembled to see me off. Some of them were smiling, trying to peer through the tinted windows of the van. As we started on our way, I held up my middle finger. I wondered if they could see me.

The day was August 21, 1995, two years after the uprising and about six months after all death row prisoners had been transferred to the Mansfield Correctional Institution (ManCI) in Mansfield, Ohio. Citing the close proximity of inmates to the execution chamber and the potential of guards forming emotional attachments with the condemned, Reginald Wilkinson, Director of the Ohio Department of Rehabilitation and Correction, thought it would be a good idea to put some distance between the opposing parties.

It was a long and torturous ride to my new home. I kept replaying the entire day over and over in my mind, wishing I could somehow reverse time. But what good would that do?

None. I cursed Judge Crow for his barely concealed racism. A miscarriage of justice had taken place inside of his courtroom and he had aided and abetted it. There had to be something I could do about it. But what? I was out of my depth, swimming in a sea of doubt and confusion. *Did I do the right thing? Should I have taken the deal?* For 147 miles I questioned myself in this way until, finally, we arrived at ManCI.

Pulling up to the prison gates, I was instantly struck by the manicured lawns and the cottage-style buildings. But for the barbed-wire fence, it could have easily been mistaken for the average college campus. Built in the early '90s, when the shift from rehabilitation to long-term incarceration began, it stood as a symbol of the new Prison Industrial Complex, where increasing numbers of the poor and underprivileged are warehoused as part of a for-profit system that actively feeds off human misery and pain. The warm and welcoming façade, as I would soon discover, was nothing more than camouflage to conceal the evil that lurked within.

When we were finally allowed through the gates, I had no idea of the hell that awaited me on the other side. As anyone in my shoes would have assumed, I thought that being sentenced to death was the "punishment" for my alleged crimes. I thought wrong. Indeed, even though I had been given the harshest penalty known to man, the State was not done with me. They had other plans.

When I stepped off the van, a black guard with the rank of captain was there to greet me. He was very cordial.

"How are you, Mr. LaMar?" he asked, smiling.

I looked at him like he was crazy.

"We've been waiting on you," he told me, as if I was checking into a hotel or something.

I looked around nervously, expecting someone to jump out and ambush me.

"How was the trip?" he continued, trying to engage me in conversation. "I bet you can't wait to get out of those cuffs...."

The more he talked, the more paranoid I became. "Listen, man, I'm not really trying to talk to you," I finally told him. He looked at me and smiled.

When we made it to RECEIVING, the cuffs were finally removed after three long hours and I rubbed my aching wrists. They were swollen and red. Then my fingerprints were taken, after which I was issued a new prison number to reflect my new conviction. I went from inmate number 210-958 to inmate number 317-117, meaning I was the 317,117th inmate to be committed into the Ohio Department of Rehabilitation and Correction. When they were done processing me, I was re-cuffed and escorted to the Death Row Unit.

Set aside and surrounded by barbed wire, the Death Row Unit was separated from the main campus: a prison within the prison. Upon entering, I stood at the beginning of a long and cold corridor.

This is it, a voice inside of me said. *If you are gonna fight these people, you gotta start now.*

When the door slammed behind me, I stopped walking.

"Let's go, LaMar," one of the guards said to me, with a puzzled expression on his face.

"I'm innocent; I didn't kill anybody," I told the guard, refusing to take another step.

"Yeah, well, you have to take that up with the courts," the captain told me. "Right now our job is to put you into a cell."

"I understand," I said, holding my ground.

When it became evident that I was not going to walk on my own, the guards began dragging me down the long corridor. It was a cruel scene: I was being dragged to my death.

"I'm innocent; I didn't do this!" I repeated, my cries echoing off the cold, concrete walls.

Finally, we made it to DR-4, the pod where I was to be housed, and I was thereupon dragged the few remaining feet to my assigned cell. Once inside, the guards removed the cuffs and slammed the cuffport before storming out of the pod in a fit of rage.

"Keith, is that you?" someone whose voice I did not recognize asked.

"Yeah, this me," I answered. "Is that you, Jason?" I guessed, having heard through the grapevine that he, too, had been sentenced to death.

"Yeah."

Jason Robb, purported leader of the Aryan Brotherhood, was the first to arrive at ManCI and, apparently, had been keeping close watch on my case and knew that I would be coming soon.

"I've been waiting on you," he told me.

We did not know each other, had never exchanged a single word, and yet, we had been thrust into this weird fraternity and somehow instinctively understood that we would have to rely on each other. Years later, after we became known as the "Lucasville Five," people would ask how it was possible for us to forge such solid bonds given that we were all so seemingly different. And the answer is simple: when you are in a burning building, factors such as race, religion, and personal background become secondary considerations once the mind shifts into survival mode.

Jason and I talked well into the night on my first day there and never once did the fact that he was in the Aryan Brotherhood come up. Instead, we talked about more immediate matters having to do with our present predicament. Instead of general population, Jason informed me, we would eventually be placed in administrative control.

"These motherfuckers are going to torture us, Keith," he told me, painting a grim picture of the road ahead.

I stood at my cell door listening, trying to wrap my mind around what he was telling me. It was hard to believe that, on top of the punishment we had already been given, we would also have to undergo what amounted to a double penalty by being thrown into solitary confinement.

A few days later, an administrator from Central Office came to speak with me and confirmed everything Jason had told me. It was a demoralizing encounter.

"And, by the way, would you prefer lethal injection or the electric chair?" he asked.

"What!"

"Yes, I have to inform you that you have the option of what method of execution you would prefer," the administrator said, pushing a piece of paper toward me with checkboxes next to the words electric chair and lethal injection.

I looked down at the paper.

"If you refuse to select one," the administrator continued, "we'll be forced to select one for you and, unfortunately, if we have to make that decision it'll be the electric chair, I'm afraid."

Never in my life had I felt so disrespected.

"Get the fuck outta my face, bitch!" I said, instinctively pulling against my restraints. "Get me the fuck out of here!" I told the guard who was overseeing this sadistic exchange.

When I abruptly stood up, the administrator jumped from his chair and moved toward the door. But he had no need to worry; I was handcuffed and shackled and bolted to the floor. Still, if it is your job to ask a man to choose between lethal injection and the electric chair, you should at least have the backbone to withstand an adverse reaction. Once again, I was reminded that "those in power do what they have the power to do, and the weak must accept what they have to accept."

Jason had warned me, but something inside me did not want to accept the grim reality of the picture he had painted. Now I had no choice but to make the necessary mental adjustments. When I made it back to the pod, Jason was looking at me with a knowing smirk on his face, one that I would come to know quite well in the years to come.

"I told you," he said.

All I could do was shake my head.

After I was there for about a week, I was contacted by my attorney, Herman Carson, who informed me that he was filing a motion for new trial after finding out that the same prosecutor, Seth Tieger, who claimed in my case that he could not provide us the names of inmates along with summaries of their statements, had turned over the very same summaries in the trial of my alleged co-defendant, Derek Cannon (*State v. Derek Cannon*, Lawrence County Court of Common Pleas, Case No. 94-CR-112). Cannon was tried immediately after me but, apparently, there was nothing preventing Tieger from complying with the law in his case.

I had no idea what this meant for me. We had caught the prosecutor with his hand in the proverbial cookie jar. But would he be held accountable for his actions?

When I found out that Judge Crow would be ruling on the motion, I was hesitant to get my hopes up. After all, it was through him that the prosecutor was allowed to violate my rights in the first place. Yet, the fact that Herman was still fighting on my behalf allowed me to be cautiously optimistic. *Some hope is better than no hope*, I reasoned.

Talking to several inmates who had been on death row for years, I was told that I should not expect to receive any relief until I reached federal court, which, if I received it at all, was 15 to 20 years away. *How in the hell will I survive that long?* I asked myself. The majority of the death row inmates I encountered seemed mentally torn down by the strain of living under the threat of death. In order to survive, most of them pretended as if what they were going through was not all that serious. "Don't Worry, Be Happy" seemed to be their motto. But I could not live this way. Whatever was in front of me, I would have to face it head on.

On September 3, 1995, Herman filed a second supplement to the motion for new trial that contained additional exculpatory evidence that had been turned over in the subsequent case of another alleged co-defendant, Rasheem Matthews (*State v. Rasheem Matthews*, Clark County Court of Common Pleas, Case No. 94-CR-742). This additional exculpatory evidence included summaries of inmates' statements that had not previously been provided to my attorneys.

For example, an inmate named Willie Kastner claimed to have witnessed the kidnapping of Bruce Vitale, one of the individuals I was convicted of killing and for whose death I had received a death sentence. According to Kastner, he and Vitale were sitting between L-3 and L-4 when an inmate named Dwitt C. "stopped and grabbed Bruce by the front of his shirt and said, 'Come with me, bitch. We have plans for you.'" This undisclosed information from Kastner implicating another inmate in the kidnapping of Bruce Vitale and the clear implication of the statement attributed to him ("we have plans for you") was favorable information that should have been disclosed in its entirety in advance of my trial to aid in the preparation of my defense.

Also attached to the second supplement was a statement by an inmate named David Hackett, who said he saw Aaron Jefferson "stabbing a white inmate in L-6."

Interestingly enough, Aaron himself admitted to killing Darrell Depina, a white inmate who was stabbed to death in L-6. I was incensed by these belated revelations. They confirmed, clearly and convincingly, that the State had withheld exculpatory evidence in my case and deprived me of a fair trial.

Finally, on October 9, 1995, we went before the Honorable Judge Crow to argue our motion. Surprisingly, he called us to Meigs County, to his hometown of Pomeroy, Ohio. Against my better judgment, I was hopeful.

He's calling us back to set things right, I told myself. *Why else is he making us travel all this way if he does not intend to grant the motion?*

I had never heard of Meigs County before, but I was not surprised when we ended up in a little town on the banks of the Ohio River. It was exactly the kind of place where someone like Judge Crow would live: an old, backward-looking town that resembled the antebellum south. Judging by the looks I received from passers-by when I emerged from the prison van, they had never seen a black man before. They gawked at me in wide-eyed wonder, as if I had just stepped off a space ship or something. Luckily, I had already been exposed to this type of thing while on trial in Ironton, Ohio. *Look straight ahead*, I reminded myself.

When I entered the jail, I was escorted under heavy guard to the holding cells in the basement. I had been on the road since early morning and was starving. When they brought my lunch tray, however, I refused to eat.

"I'm good," I told the deputy, certain that they had taken the opportunity to spit in my food.

"What? Our food ain't good enough for you?" the deputy asked.

"Not hungry," I lied.

Around noon, I was taken up to an anteroom to meet

with my attorney. Although Herman and I had stayed in touch, it had been a couple of months since we had last seen each other. He was standing up when I came into the room, holding a stack of legal books under one arm. With the other arm, he reached out to give me a hug.

"How you doin', Herman?" I asked, leaning into his chest and laying my head on his shoulder. I would have hugged him in kind, but I was still handcuffed and shackled.

"Did you eat something?" he asked, giving me one last squeeze before releasing me from his grasp.

I shook my head no.

"No? They said you were having lunch."

I smiled and sat down. I was ready to get on with it. I had not come to Meigs County to eat; I had come to find out whether or not I would receive a new trial.

"So, tell me, what are my chances, man?" I asked, getting down to business.

"It's hard to say, Keith," he said, turning serious. "They clearly violated your rights; but whether or not Judge Crow will agree with us, who can say?"

I nodded my head in understanding. Yeah, who but the judge could say?

Shortly thereafter, we were sitting before His Honor, who was perched atop his pedestal, looking dense as ever. He glanced over in my direction and looked straight through me, as if I was invisible. What little optimism I had began to fade in the face of such impenetrable ignorance and bigotry. I looked over to the prosecutor's table and glared at Seth Tieger, who seemed to have taken the most joy in depriving me of my rights. He sat there peering down his nose with the usual pompous expression on his face, secure in the knowledge that he was beyond reproach.

When things got underway, Herman stood up and argued in support of our motion. He pointed out that the very same summaries that had been so highly contested during my trial were turned over in the trial of Derek Cannon, my alleged co-defendant. Furthermore, the same attorney, Seth Tieger, who previously claimed the statements were obtained through promises of confidentiality, prosecuted Cannon.

What the State did to us in this case is put us in a situation where we had a Sunday puzzle, one of those Sunday puzzles where you have column A with names and column B with statements, and you mix and match and try to find which ones adjoin that corresponding name.

Now, *Brady vs. Maryland* does not allow for that. That's a United States Supreme Court case this Court is familiar with. *Brady vs. Maryland* puts a duty on the prosecution, an obligation that they must provide us with names. It's not the Court's responsibility. It's the prosecutor's responsibility; and in this particular case, they failed to do it as they did in the Cannon and Matthews case[s]. They could have done it. They did it there. They did not do it in our case, and we were harmed and harmed to our prejudice.

When he finished his impassioned argument, Herman sat down next to me. His hands were trembling.

"That was good, Herman," I said, swelling with pride that he had argued so vigorously on my behalf.

"Thanks, Keith," he said, visibly shaken by the force of his indignation.

Even Judge Crow seemed moved by what he had heard. He questioned first Herman and then the prosecutor about what had been disclosed in the subsequent trials.

Sensing a sudden shift in current, Prosecutor Tieger defended his actions by blaming us for not properly investigating the case:

> They had three months with all these names and all these statements. They had an investigator. They could have gone to every prison and talked to every one of those people; and only until Keith LaMar is convicted and things didn't go their way, well, that's when they come back to you and say it was an impossibility to do. They had ample opportunity to do it if it was true, and they didn't do it.

"Alright," Judge Crow responded, "the Court is going to overrule that motion and make the findings as outlined by the State."

Hearing this, Herman abruptly stood up:

> For the record, I'm not going to let what Mr. Tieger said just now go unanswered. It is one thing to have been given nothing more than a name of a witness and go to that witness on a fishing trip. It is another thing to go in and tell them, look, I've got this statement that you gave, so we know who you've already implicated. It is a totally different situation.

> The ruling of the Court sent us forth totally unarmed to interview this list of witnesses. We didn't even know what we were there to ask them about, because we didn't have the statements matched up to the names like they got in Mr. Matthews' case and Mr. Cannon's case.

Again, it was an impassioned plea. After further back and forth, Herman made one last attempt to explain to Judge Crow the inconsistency between the court's ruling and what *Brady* requires:

Brady vs. Maryland doesn't say that the State is to give us hints, riddles and puzzles to solve. It says that they are to give us exculpatory evidence.

What Herman said cut to the very crux of the injustice that occurred, and he was asking the judge to remedy his erroneous application of *Brady* by granting us a new trial. Indeed, it was the only equitable thing to do.

But did he do it? Of course not; his pride and prejudice forbade it.

Without further ado, Judge Crow stood by his earlier ruling and succinctly dashed all of my hopes.

"Okay. The Court is going to overrule the motion [and] order the State to prepare the entry."

He then immediately got up from the bench and hurriedly made his way toward the exit, which just so happened to be next to the defense table where I was now standing. Just as he was about to cross my path, he looked into my eyes and said, "Good luck, Keith." And then he was gone.

I was devastated. Having my life in the hands of someone so heartless killed my spirit and left me speechless. I shuffled out of the courtroom like a zombie, detached from my surroundings, disconnected from my thoughts and feelings—a dead man walking.

As I made my way across the courtyard, the October sun shone down in unseasonable warmth. I kept walking toward the prison van, wanting so badly to be free of this place. And then I heard my name, "Keith!" When I turned around, I saw

Herman a short distance away with his stack of legal books under his arm, waving goodbye. I could see the deep disappointment on his face. He shared my pain. I raised my head to signal goodbye, too hurt to speak and blinded by the tears that were forming in my eyes....

When I made it back to the prison and walked into the pod (after once again being dragged down the long corridor), Jason was standing at his cell door with an expectant look on his face. After the guards left, a light tap sounded on my cell wall.

"Yeah?" I answered.

"What's up, man; what'd they do?" he wanted to know.

I was not in the mood for a long, drawn out conversation.

"He overruled it, Jason," I told him, matter-of-factly.

"Oh, yeah? Did he—"

"Listen, man, I'll talk to you later, alright? I'm about to crash out."

"Yeah, okay; I hear you."

I slept for three days straight.

When I woke up, I found a note on the cell floor. I unfolded and read it:

> In this world, where the game is played with loaded dice, a man must have a temper of iron, with armor proof to the blows of fate, and weapons to make his way against men. Life is one long battle; we have to fight at every step; and Voltaire very rightly says that if we succeed, it is at the point of the sword, and that we die with the weapon in our hand.
>
> —Arthur Schopenhauer

I had never heard of the author of the quote but his words instantly struck a chord in me and coaxed me out of my stupor. I tapped on the wall.

"Yeah," Jason immediately responded, as if he had been standing there waiting on me.

"I read that," I told him, looking down at the piece of paper in my hand. "Who is Arthur Schopenhauer?" I asked.

"He's a philosopher from Germany," he told me. "You like that, huh?"

"Yeah, yeah—it's cool. I mean, it's true. This shit is one long battle, man," I said, wiping sleep from my eyes. "And what about this cat, Voltaire—who's that?"

"Oh, he's pretty slick. I have one of his books over here if you want to check it out," he offered.

"Yeah, I'll check it out. Is it any good?"

"Check it out and see," he told me.

So I did. The book was called *Candide*, a story about a young man who sets out on a journey and encounters all kinds of trials and tribulations. It was an excellent book and I was grateful to Jason for having shared it with me.

"Cultivate your garden," the protagonist was repeatedly reminded. I thought deeply about what that meant and, with inexperienced tools, resolved to cultivate my own garden. But first, before anything, there was still a bit of sadness to endure and conquer.

On October 15, 1995, six days after Judge Crow denied the motion for new trial, my grandfather died. He was the most important person in my life and news of his death gutted me, left me feeling empty and alone. A few days before he passed away, I had spoken to him on the telephone, unaware that it would be the last time we would speak to each other. He was suffering from emphysema, a disease that sapped him of his strength and left him confined to what would literally become his deathbed. To spare him the pain of my ordeal, I had intentionally avoided talking to him. *Knowing I'm facing the death penalty would kill him,* I thought. But he was an eternal optimist, my grandfather, and even after he found out that I had been convicted of multiple murders and placed on death row, he used what turned out to be his last breaths to encourage me to wake up and live.

"You gotta be strong, Keith," he told me. "You know, life doesn't have to be so hard, grandson; you don't have to be so tough."

"I know, granddad," I said.

"You see, all that pain you have inside you, you have to let it go. It's not worth it."

"I'll try, granddad." Tears were welling up in my eyes.

"You wake up one day and your whole life—"

"So when are you coming to see me?" I interrupted, trying to change the conversation.

He had never spoken to me in this way before, had never once hinted at the pain he felt over not being able to reach me, and now he was trying to get me to take a good look at myself.

"Oh, this life, grandson," he went on, "it can be so good to you if you would just take it easy and go slow. You don't have to always be going around trying to prove yourself to everybody."

"I know, granddad," I said, feeling a bit defensive. "I'm not trying to—"

"Listen! I need you to listen to me, Keith," he demanded.

"I'm listening, granddad."

Tears were streaming down my face and I was doing everything in my power to hold it together.

"I'm sorry for letting you down, granddad," I tried to say through my tears.

"You didn't let me down, son," he said. "We do the best we can and—"

"You have 60 seconds left on this call," the automated

operator cut in, reminding me that I had lost complete control of my life.

"And sometimes that's all we can do, my friend," he finished saying. "So just do the best you can, okay?"

"I will, granddad."

"Okay. And I love you, Keith."

"I love you, too, granddad," I rushed to add, praying that the phone would not cut off before I had the opportunity to say what I was feeling.

"Okay, baby," he said, chuckling into the receiver.

And then the phone went dead.

I walked back to the cell in a daze, feeling as if I had just awakened from a dream. When the door slammed behind me, I sat down on the bed and cried. How could I have been so blind and naïve as to believe that my life belonged to me and me alone?

Seized by the guilt and pain that only understanding can bring, I rushed to the cell door and called to the guard in hopes that I could convince him to allow me to make one last call. I wanted to talk to my grandfather again. I wanted to tell him that I finally understood and that he did not have to worry about me anymore. But such was not to be. I had already made my monthly phone call, I was told, and, ironically, the only way for me to qualify for an "emergency call" was upon my grandfather's passing. But it would be too late by then. I turned away from the door and walked back to the bed, broken.

For days, weeks, I stumbled around in the deepest darkness I had ever known, trying to find something in the memory of my experiences that could help me comprehend the pain I was in. But nothing came; indeed, what I was going through was unprecedented. In the space and span of just a few months, I had lost both my grandparents and had been sentenced to death. Indeed, my whole world had been turned upside down, leaving me without a frame of reference from which to draw. My grandfather told me to be strong, but where could I find such strength? He asked me to let go of my pain, but how? What had been done to me was wrong, criminally unjust, and it filled me with a hate and rage that boiled my blood.

By the end of October, a third man by the name of Namir Abdul Mateen (formerly known as James Were) arrived on death row. Like Jason, he had been given the death penalty for his alleged involvement in the slaying of Officer Vallandingham. According to the State, a meeting between inmate leaders was held on April 15, 1993, wherein a vote was taken to determine whether or not a guard should be killed. Now the "leaders" of this alleged meeting were being singled out for retribution.

After Namir, George Skatzes, one of the alleged leaders of the Aryan Brotherhood, arrived. He was followed by Siddique Abdullah Hasan (formerly known as Carlos Sanders), the purported leader of the Sunni Muslims and suspected "mastermind" of the uprising.

Along with everyone else, I was eager to meet Hasan. We had crossed paths only once before, but it was a brief encounter that left a lasting impression on me. We were walking L-side corridor one day, heading in opposite directions, when my beaded necklace broke and scattered all over the hallway. Without introducing himself or waiting to be asked, he got down on his knees and helped me retrieve the 99 beads. "Have a good day, my brotha," he said, after we were done with the task. In an environment where kindness was routinely mistaken for weakness, I was duly impressed by the deed. In the years to come, as we found ourselves embroiled in battle after battle against the powers that be, I would find other occasions to be impressed.

Now that we were all firmly in place, the administration wasted no time in making good on their promise to put us on administrative control. Without notice, or the slightest pretense of due process, they came and took away all our personal belongings, leaving us with only the bare essentials: toothbrush, underwear, socks, T-shirts, and so on. They also took the phone off the wall and started holding our outgoing mail, making it virtually impossible for us to stay connected to the outside world. We did not know it at the time, but this marked the beginning of a more than two-decades-long stint in solitary confinement.

Shutting off phone access was critical in keeping us incommunicado. If we could not communicate with our attorneys or our families, no one would know about the conditions we were being subjected to.

In response to our mounting frustrations, we all decided that the best course of action would be to go on a hunger strike, which hopefully would attract some outside attention and thereby put an end to the maltreatment we were experiencing.

After about a week of not eating, someone from the administration met with us and, by promising immediate changes, convinced us to discontinue our protest. Against our better judgment, we ended the strike. However, instead of things getting better, they got worse.

George Skatzes began having serious problems with his stomach. On top of everything else we were already enduring, his sudden illness caused us to believe that our food was being poisoned. Thus, in response to our suspicions, I started eating only raw fruits and vegetables. Soon I began having very vivid nightmares of being executed, strapped to a gurney with poison pumping through my veins. The dreams got so bad that I woke up to the shocking pain of my fists punching the wall, striking out at my nameless, faceless executioners. Months of uncertainty passed wherein we filed complaints and grievances, but they failed to effect the desired changes.

After another year had passed, it was clear that we had to do something. However, when talk of another hunger strike came up, I immediately resisted the suggestion.

"Ain't no way I'm doin' that again," I interjected, thinking about the intense pain I had felt after only one week of starving myself. "They ain't gonna do nothing but lie to us again," I said.

In spite of my strenuous objections, the discussion continued as though I had said nothing. Feeling slighted and outnumbered, I voiced the opinion that, "Instead of the Lucasville Five, we should be called the Lucasville Four," referring to the obvious alliances between Namir and Hasan (the two Muslims), and George and Jason (the two Aryans). It was an unwarranted statement; from the very beginning we had all taken pains to treat each other with the utmost respect. Still, sensing my sour state of mind, George rushed to reassure me that no such divisions existed.

"You're not in this by yourself, Bomani," he told me. "We're all in this together."

"Okay," I relented, giving my assent. "But, listen, if we're going on another hunger strike, we have to go all the way this time," I warned, thinking about how we had been duped.

Everybody agreed.

None of us really knew what "all the way" meant. From somewhere, we had somehow gathered the impression that if we stopped eating for three weeks or lost more than 20 pounds (whichever came first) that the administration would be forced to put us under medical supervision, which, in the long run, would cost them more trouble than the situation was worth. There was some talk of being force-fed, but none of us fully appreciated how painful such a procedure would actually be, or whether any of us could make it to that point. As before, we were laboring under delusions.

Shortly after the third week had elapsed and we were all well beyond the 20-pound mark, I was placed under medical supervision due to my low blood sugar levels. Every hour, on the hour, a nurse was summoned to my cell to check my vital signs to make sure I was still lucid.

It's working, I remember thinking to myself, convinced that our strategy was proceeding as planned. But after being awakened from my sleep hour after hour all through the night, I began to have second thoughts. We were approaching the fourth week and the administration still showed no signs of yielding. It never occurred to us that they were perfectly willing to sit back and watch us starve ourselves to death. Finally, unable to wait any longer, I drafted a letter to the warden:

Mr. Ralph Coyle
Mansfield Correctional Inst.
P.O. Box 788
Mansfield, Ohio 44901

July 14, 1997
Re: HUNGER STRIKE

Mr. Coyle (et al.):

This letter is in regards to the reasons we have elected to initiate a strike in order to protest against the unfair conditions that we have been subjected to since being convicted and sentenced to death and subsequently confined here at the Mansfield Correctional Institution.

Sir, as you know, we have consistently communicated with Mr. Israel concerning this matter, but as of this date, there still seems to be some confusion with respect to our concerns and expectations. Therefore, to guard against further waste of each other's time, we all agreed that it would be more conducive to reaching a resolution if we simply stated our position, thereby giving you the opportunity to clearly consider the issues involved...

To begin with, we already understand that there are some concerns regarding security, and that due to the nature of the circumstances that resulted in us being placed on death row, it falls within your responsibility to enforce whatever "Security" measures you deem necessary. Understanding that, we recognize your need to keep us in an isolated area. However, as we have repeatedly attempted to explain, keeping us in an isolated area and denying us the privileges that do not constitute a security threat is equivalent to punishing us twice for the same offense.

At the forefront of our list of concerns, we are asking that George Skatzes receive immediate medical attention for what is, as yet, an undiagnosed problem he's been having with his stomach. With respect to this, he has repeatedly tried, to no avail, to have the doctor order some tests in order to determine what the problem is. Surely he is entitled to the same attention that is accorded to everyone else, and we're asking that he be given the attention capable of addressing these concerns and preventing his problem from becoming any worse than what it already is.

Secondly, with regards to the privileges, we're asking that we be given "all" our personal property that doesn't interfere with you maintaining security.

As this is a security issue, we're asking that we be accorded the same privileges that were given to all SOCF inmates immediately following the riot and placed on Security Control Investigation here at the Mansfield Correctional Institution.

Those privileges consist of:

1) All personal property (TV, typewriter, etc.)

2) Access to phones

3) Food Boxes (no can goods per institutional policy)

4) Full commissary privileges

5) Full visitation privileges

6) Full recreational privileges

7) Legal services

8) Stop messing with our mail

Enclosed, please find the "exact" Commissary list that was provided to those inmates placed on SECURITY CONTROL. Also, we're enclosing a copy of the so-called "21-point agreement."[9] Of particular importance, in our opinion, are #2 and #14, which state that: There will be no retaliating actions taken toward any inmates or their property! If you will take the time to investigate, you'll find that we have presented no problems since being

---

[9] The agreement that ended the Lucasville Uprising in a peaceful surrender. See www.keithlamar.org to review the document.

here. The only problem exists in us being singled out and treated contrary to everyone else. This, we are no longer willing to accept.

Finally, we ask that you acknowledge the urgency in addressing our concerns, as this is approaching the fourth week of the strike and we have no intention of yielding until we receive a legitimate response and appropriate changes are made.

Sincerely,

George Skatzes
Jason Robb
S. A. Hasan
James Were
Keith LaMar

Although I should have expected as much, I was deeply disappointed when, after a few days had gone by, we still had not received a reply from the warden. This upset me. We were starving ourselves to receive what other similarly situated inmates already had. Yet the administration seemed in no rush to accommodate us. Were they trying to bait us into doing something rash? George and Hasan seemed to believe so. They both cautioned against doing anything that would play into their hands. I heard what they had to say and it seemed perfectly plausible that the administration was stalling in order to lure us into a trap.

"Let's stay focused," George suggested, encouraging each of us to "keep our eyes on the prize." In the meantime, my blood sugar level was steadily dropping and, on top of that, I had developed a bleeding ulcer from living under so much strain.

"I'm done," I announced one morning, feeling physically and mentally depleted.

"C'mon, Bomani," Namir implored, using what little strength he had left to persuade me to stay in the game.

But my mind was made up. I had gone as far as I was willing to go and, though it pained me to let them down, we had agreed to make our own decisions about whether or not to continue. I told them that I was tired of slowly killing myself, tired of begging and pleading to be treated like a human being.

"Why should we have to starve ourselves to receive the same things that other death row inmates already have?" I asked.

As things stood, we could not even participate in our own appeals. How could we when we were not even allowed to use the telephone or go to the law library to research our cases? This is what angered me the most. As a death row inmate, you only get one shot to present the pertinent issues and make them part of the record. If you do not have at least a fundamental understanding of the law and how the process works, it is virtually impossible to know if this is being done. However, instead of familiarizing ourselves with this most critical stage of the process, we were starving ourselves to death.

"I'm done with this shit!" I repeated with finality.

Shortly thereafter, the strike came to an end. Though no one said anything, I felt a sense of responsibility for our collective failure. We had gone through all of that pain and suffering for nothing—for *nothing!* To keep from feeling the shame that came with being defeated, I turned inward and stopped talking. Indeed, there was nothing left to say.

About a month or so later, after I had regained my strength, I was struck by a jolt of inspiration. While recuperating from the rigors of the strike, I poured over Frantz Fanon's *The Wretched of the Earth*, which, among other things, delved deeply into the science of using violence as a way to regain one's humanity. Naturally, given the circumstances I found myself in, I responded very much to the idea that, by utilizing my own agency, I could change the conditions of my life. To this end, I fashioned a knife out of a piece of steel and smuggled it outside. When no one was watching, I placed it inside the backboard of the basketball hoop. It was still there on September 5, 1997, when I came outside and decided to make my move.

It was a sunny day and relief officers (who were notorious for not following protocol), were running the pod. Seeing this, I asked one of the inmate porters to take the basketball out of the rec cage and place it in the hallway. When the time was right, I would use this as a pretext to get the cage door reopened.

At dinnertime, when the guards were in the middle of overseeing the inmate porters hand out the evening meal, I set my plan in motion.

"Hey, C.O.," I called out, hoping to pull one of the guards away from the desk. When no one responded, I called out again, "Hey, C.O! Hey, C.O!"

Hearing me yell, one of the guards peeked around the bend in the hallway to see what all of the ruckus was about.

"I need the basketball!" I yelled impatiently, gesturing with my arms. One of the guards got up from the desk and started moving in my direction.

When he was within earshot, I repeated my request. "Could you roll me that basketball, man?" I asked, pointing. He turned around and looked at the basketball and then looked back at me. He was thinking about it. Seeing his hesitation, I stepped away from the cage door to let him see that it would be easier—and quicker—if he would just open the cage and roll the basketball in to me. When he turned and started walking away, I thought he was going to blow me off. Then he stopped and picked up the ball.

I felt for the knife in the waistband of my sweatpants and took a deep breath. My heart was pounding out of my chest. *Be cool, be cool,* I told myself, trying to steady my nerves.

I had already resolved not to hurt anyone. My sole purpose was to demolish the pod, to make it unlivable, and thereby force the administration to transfer me out-of-state. Where did I get this idea? It was one of the stipulations agreed upon during the negotiations that brought an end to the Lucasville Uprising. In fact, several inmates, believing they would be subject to endless retaliation, had already taken advantage of the opportunity to relocate, and I was hoping to do the same.

Understandably, some people believe that by doing what I was about to do I confirmed what the State said about me. But these people have no idea what it feels like to be trapped inside a cell 24 hours a day, on death row, for something they did not do. They have never experienced the horror of watching an otherwise healthy individual slip into schizophrenic behavior and start smearing his own feces all over his body. They do not know the dread involved in being in an environment where perfectly sane individuals snap and take their own lives. And it was this—the fear of losing my mind—that drove me to try to do something about the hell that I was living in.

When the guard opened the cage to roll the basketball inside, I grabbed the knife from the waistband of my sweatpants and stormed through the door, knocking him to the ground. A second guard, who was standing in the doorway leading into the building, took off running, dropping his keys in the process. I picked up the keys and went after him. When I caught up to him, I grabbed his arm and pressed the knife into his side.

"Don't be no hero, man," I told him, turning him around so that he was facing the wall. "I ain't trying to hurt nobody,"

I assured him, before grabbing the cuffs from his belt and handcuffing him behind his back. I then walked him to a conference room that was near the door leading outside. After putting him inside, I could hear the other guard fumbling with his keys in the lock, trying to lock himself outside. I immediately snatched the door open and grabbed him, forcing him face-first against the wall.

"I'm not gonna hurt you, man," I told him, pulling the cuffs from his belt and handcuffing him behind his back. After moving him into the conference room and closing the door behind me, I made my way to the torture chamber that had been my home for the past 18 months.

Inside the pod, a third guard was busy passing out laundry. He stood in the middle of the fenced-in stairwell holding a laundry bag. The fence itself had a door built onto it that could be locked, but which had been left open while the guard went up and down the stairs (another breach of protocol). When he noticed me standing at the door trying to get into the pod, he ran to the bottom of the stairwell intent on locking the door. However, in his panic-stricken state, he was apparently unable to find the right key and fumbled frantically with the lock. Meanwhile, I was engaged in my own frantic search, trying to find the right key to the pod door. A serious comedy ensued: who would be the first to find the magic key?

After the first key did not work, I tried another one, then another, looking up intermittently to see if the guard would beat me to the punch. And then I found the right one. When I opened the door, the guard took off running up the stairs. I ran after him. When I caught up to him, I fell on his back and grabbed the walkie-talkie to prevent the "man-down" signal from activating.

"Don't fuck me!" the guard screamed out in exaggerated pain, as if I had removed his pants instead of his walkie-talkie. Even under the circumstances, it was an odd exclamation, especially coming from a man who never passed on the opportunity to be sadistic.

"I'm not gonna fuck you," I said, disgusted by his weird reaction. I reached for his handcuffs and secured his hands behind his back. "Get your tough ass up," I told him, thinking about all the times he had thrown away my mail or in some other way deprived me of what I was entitled to. If I were going to hurt anyone, it would have been him; he deserved it. But as I had done with the others, I walked him to the conference room and locked him inside. I then returned to the pod and unlocked all the cell doors.

"Let's tear this mothafucka up!" I shouted, already feeling victorious. I then made my way to the other side of the pod, where the so-called "good" death row inmates were housed, and unlocked the doors.

"Let's tear this mothafucka up!" I repeated. Within a few short minutes, we were standing in the middle of a disaster area. All the windows had been busted out and the mini-kitchen and office area were destroyed.

In the meantime, the guards who had been locked inside the conference room were "rescued" by a fellow officer who happened upon the scene during a routine security check. I saw the officers being pulled out of the pod and was strangely relieved that they were no longer in harm's way. After all, it was impossible to know what would happen to them with all the inmates out of their cells. But now they were gone.

Good, I thought. The last thing I wanted was to create a situation during which another guard or inmate was killed. True, I was in a desperate state of mind, but I was not blind to the consequences of someone losing his life; if that happened, I would be held responsible. Hence, I remained vigilant. And it was a good thing I did.

In the heat of the moment, several inmates who were awaiting execution dates tried to kill an inmate named Wilford Berry, who had voluntarily forfeited his appeals, and twice I had to pull them off him, even as he himself begged to be killed.

"Please kill me!" he pleaded, through bloodstained teeth. It was the saddest thing I had ever seen. He was asking to be taken out of his misery, to be spared the pain of waking up another day in a place where his soul was constantly ravaged by the memory of his crimes.

Thinking about it now, as I write this, brings to mind a question once posed by Kahlil Gibran, [10] who asked, "How shall you punish those whose remorse is already greater than their misdeeds?"

By voluntarily forfeiting his appeals, Berry was unwittingly setting into motion the machinery of death in Ohio. He was perfectly within his rights in giving up the power to challenge his convictions; after all, a man can do whatever he wants to with his own life. I believe that. However, at the time, the State of Ohio had not executed anyone since 1963.

In fact, the death penalty was briefly suspended in the United States due to a Supreme Court ruling in the 1970s. But even after the drafting of a new law in 1981 that made it permissible for the State of Ohio to kill again, no inmate had yet to feel the sting of the executioner's needle. Many inmates believed that Berry's decision to be the "Volunteer" (as he was called) would open up the floodgates and clear the way for other inmates to be executed.[11] Therefore, they

---

[10] Kahlil Gibran, "On Crime and Punishment," *The Prophet* (Alfred A. Knopf, 1923).

[11] Since 1999, the year Wilford Berry's voluntary death was carried out, 53 men have been executed in Ohio.

tried to kill him, believing it would somehow stop the machine.

After about two hours, and after we had already demolished the pod, we noticed a battalion of guards assembled outside the building.

Here we go again, I mumbled to myself, recalling the uprising of 1993.

A short time later, a phone inside the pod began to ring. It was a negotiator. *A negotiator?*

"Hey, look, this is not a hostage situation; the guards were immediately let go," I told the woman on the other end of the phone. "It's over; we're ready to go back to our cells."

"Well, that certainly sounds good," the negotiator said, breathing what sounded like a sigh of relief. And then, after a brief pause: "Listen, we want you guys to file into the recreation area inside the pod and wait there."

"For what?" I asked, bewildered. "I said we're ready to go back to our cells."

Silence.

"Hello? Hello?" I called.

"Yeah, we need you to file into the recreation area." It was a man's voice now.

I hung up the phone. Something was not right.

"Why would they want us to squeeze into the rec cage?" I asked Jason, furrowing my brow.

"Yeah, that doesn't sound right," he said. "Let's just lock up in our cells."

With that, Jason went around and made sure that everyone's door was on "automatic," meaning each door, once closed, would automatically lock on its own without a key. Looking back, I am convinced that this move saved my life.

Once we all went back to our cells and locked the doors, we assumed that the worst was over. Yes, unfortunately, some people had been hurt, but no one had been killed. Whatever the consequences, I was prepared to face them, especially if it meant I would be sent to a prison out-of-state. But once again, as always, the State had other plans.

As George and Hasan had suspected, the authorities had been waiting for just such a situation. It did not matter that no one was killed or that we were already back in our cells. The State wanted to exact revenge—not so much for the present situation, but because of what had happened in 1993. Their desire for retribution is why we were placed in an isolated area, set apart from the other death row inmates. I see it so clearly now: the unnecessary restrictions, the constant lies and deprivation—it was all calculated and designed to push us into making an impulsive move.

You can call it a premonition or just plain good luck, but something told me not to go back to my assigned cell. Instead, I stayed on the other side with the "good" death row inmates. I hunkered down with two old-timers, a pair of solid cats who had been on death row for over a decade by then. They had both already exhausted their appeals and were nearing execution. I no longer remember the details of how I ended up in the cell with them, but, though they are both dead now, I owe them an apology for crawling all over them after the authorities broke the window out and shot teargas into the cell.

This is why I say Jason saved my life: had he not thought to put the automatic lock on the doors, I would have run out of the cell and given the authorities, who had entered the building armed with shotguns and wearing gas masks, justification to gun me down. But, thankfully, I was not gunned down. In fact, by the time the smoke cleared, I was sitting safely inside the warehouse with nothing more than a few scratches on my arms and legs.

Jason was not so lucky. He went back to his assigned cell

and the "goon squad" beat him nearly half to death. They cracked his skull, broke his ribs, and put two huge lacerations atop both his eyes that required 36 stitches to close. When I next saw him, I did not even recognize him, he had been beaten so badly.

"Sorry, man," I said to him a few weeks later. I felt guilty. Because of my actions, he had almost lost his life.

"For what?" he asked, genuinely perplexed.

"For almost getting you killed, man" I replied. "I shouldn't have done that stupid shit, but I was losing my mind, Jason."

"Well, they say you gotta lose your mind in order to find it. Did you find it?" he asked, smiling.

"Find what?"

"Your mind."

"I think so. I think I can see this shit more clearly now," I tried to assure him.

"Good. 'Cause they'll be coming for you soon, Bomani."

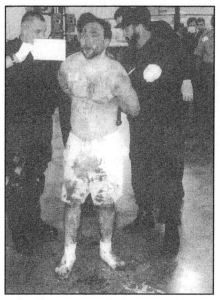

Jason Robb, after he was beaten by the goon squad

And he was right. A couple of months later the goon squad came for me. I was sitting on the bed reading when the cuffport was opened and I was sprayed with Mace. I was caught totally off guard.

When I got up from the bed to see what was going on, there were 20 or so guards dressed in black standing in front of my cell in full riot gear. A lone "white shirt"—a certain Lieutenant Young—stood among the sea of black. He was known for being extremely cruel and vicious. I stilled myself when I saw him. I had only recently read in the institution's administrative rules (or "ARs") that "deadly force" could be used if, during a cell extraction, an inmate puts forth any resistance. This crossed my mind as I stood there.

Are they going to kill me? I wondered, frantically looking around the cell for something I could use as a weapon. But there was nothing. And then Lieutenant Young, with video camera in hand, gave me a direct order:

LY: LaMar, I need you to step forward and cuff up.

Me: [nervously] No problem.

LY: Please be advised that inmate LaMar is refusing a direct order to put on the handcuffs.

Me: [raising my voice so that those around me could hear that I was complying with the rules] I said I would cuff up!

LY: [continuing, unperturbed] Yes, we are about to perform a cell extraction of inmate LaMar for refusing a direct order.

Me: [screaming at the top of my lungs] I said I would cuff up!

LY: [with a smirk on his face] LaMar, please step away from the door and get down on your knees.

Seeing the futility in arguing, I stepped away from the door. But I refused to get down on my knees. If it were indeed their plan to kill me, I would die on my feet. I would fight them.

When Lieutenant Young saw that I was prepared to fight, he opened the slot and sprayed me with Mace. When one can was empty, he called for another one, and then another. By the time he was done spraying me, I could barely breathe, let alone put up any resistance. Seeing that I was on the verge of collapse, the goon squad rushed into the cell and beat me to my knees, put the handcuffs on me, and then beat me some more. When I was flat on the floor, a black guard, who seemed intent on causing me the most pain, sat down on my back, grabbed my head between his hands and pounded it on the cement floor. I lost consciousness.

I came to in the hallway outside the pod. I had no idea how I had gotten there, but somehow I had made it down a flight of stairs without walking. Now I was being held up so that each of them could land a proper blow to my face, stomach, and crotch.

My left eye was swollen completely closed, but I could still see them. I saw the strained expressions on their faces as they tried with all their might to hurt me. They wanted me to cry out in pain. But I was not in pain. I felt nothing. Indeed, I had left my body and was watching them from a curious distance.

Who is that being beaten? I wondered. And then I lost consciousness again.

I woke up in a strip cell and found myself naked. Slowly, as I came back to my senses, pain cascaded down my body like burning lava. My whole body was on fire. Gradually, the pain subsided and I was able to touch myself: my eyes, my lips, my penis.

They tried to kill me. And what happened to my clothes, why am I naked?

As night fell, the temperature inside the cell dropped to almost zero. I pounded on the cell door to see if I could get a guard to come, but no one answered. Finally, desperate for the slightest bit of warmth, I tore a hole in the mattress and crawled inside.

The next day, when the guards saw that I had crawled into the mattress, they confiscated it and left me in handcuffs and shackles for most of the day, freezing to the bone. I did not realize it at first, but the cell I was in had a camera embedded in the door; they were watching me. They watched me for three whole days before they gave me some clothing, a mattress and some sheets. I lay down and went to sleep. I slept for days, weeks, and no one, including my closest friends and family, knew where I was.

The following is a letter Marianne Kruse-Blanchong, Ohio Coordinator for the Death Row Support Project, sent to Warden Coyle inquiring about my whereabouts and well-being:

10 November 1997

Warden Coyle—MANCI
PO Box 788
Mansfield, OH 44901

Dear Warden Coyle,

Man can break the fragile thread in any environment when violence is introduced, and I fear that fragile thread is being broken by the constant beatings that the men in the environment of your death row are experiencing.

Not but a few months ago there was an uprising where men on a block were beaten, and afterwards a guard was terminated. I have since received letters from several inmates expressing their fears and concerns over the most recent incident, which occurred on Friday October 31st, 1997.

A Lt. Young, who is employed in the property room, entered LC Unit 5 B and, for no reason, opened the food hatch of Mr. Keith LaMar's cell and sprayed him with an aerosol Mace. No one heard Mr. LaMar resist or respond in a violent manner that would warrant a beating. Then, to add insult to injury, Sgt. Clark filled out his paper work in favor of Lt. Young's actions by stating that Mr. LaMar refused to be cuffed.

Why did Lt. Young go to Mr. LaMar's cell in the first place?

Mr. LaMar has not been returned to his cell and his whereabouts is unknown, which adds to the concern of the other inmates....

...The 174 men within the environment of your death row are human beings, not animals. To be locked in a cell and not know when your food hatch is opened if you will be the next one to be mazed [sic] and beaten can result in a very stressful situation that constitutes cruel and unusual punishment.

Please stop that fragile thread from breaking. Only you can investigate and stop the needless violence of maltreatment and abuse...

Respectfully,

Marianne Kruse-Blanchong
Ohio Coordinator, Death Row Support Project

Another posting by advocates, inquiring about my whereabouts, asked:

Where is Keith LaMar and Whatever Happened to Human Rights in America?
Ohio Prisoner Rights Advocates Want Factual Answers to These and Other Probing Questions.

Information has reached this advocate from two reliable sources that Keith LaMar of Mansfield Death Row was brutally beaten by correctional officers on Oct 31.

During separate conversations with Sonny Williams of the Ohio Prisoners' Rights Union and Marianne Kruse-Blanchong of the Ohio Death Row Support Project, it was learned that Keith LaMar's food hatch door was opened by a Lt. Young (who does not work DR but is assigned to property room duty) and pepper spray and/or gas was used on him. He was forcibly removed from his cell after being "subdued" by this Lt. (and possibly others) and his whereabouts since then are unknown. Keith LaMar is the supposed instigator of the Mansfield DR Uprising of Sept 5.

Marianne Kruse-Blanchong reports that today, Nov 8, 1997, she received a letter from DR prisoner David Sneed that stated LaMar had offered no resistance, had provoked no one, and that the regular DR guards and a Sgt. Clark had backed up Lt. Young's story.

Question: if it is fact that Lt. Young is not usually assigned to DR, why was he in this section of the prison and why was he allowed access to Keith Lamar? Where is Keith Lamar?

Where was I? Rumor had it that I was transferred out-of-state to the supermax prison in Florence, Colorado. Some had it that I was in the intensive care unit at the local hospital, clinging to life. In point of fact, however, I was holed up in DR-1, a pod within the very same building where I was originally housed. I would stay there until my swollen eyes, busted lips and bruised ribs healed. In the meantime, I would be held incommunicado, prevented from using the telephone or sending letters out to my friends and family.

Eventually, through an inmate who was in the pod with me, I was able to get a message out to my attorney, Herman Carson, who contacted the warden on my behalf and questioned him as to why I was being subjected to such harsh treatment. The warden lied and said I had thrown urine on a guard and then refused to come out of my cell to face disciplinary action. Though blatantly false, this was the excuse that was supplied to justify the beating and subsequent torment that I had endured.

I realize that it may sound as if I am complaining, but I am merely explaining what happened. I am not without the awareness that points to the part I played in bringing about my own hurt and pain. In this, James Baldwin was most certainly correct when he said, "Hatred, which could destroy so much, never failed to destroy the man who hated."

Indeed, I was filled with hate after all that had been done to me, and I was fighting in the only way that I knew how. It did not occur to me at the time that I was caught up in a process of self-destruction. I was in agony, mourning the loss of my grandparents, the loss of my own life, and trying desperately to find my way back to myself. Yet, the more I struggled and the more pressure I applied, the deeper I seemed to sink into the madness.

By the time I made it back to Jason, Hasan, Namir and George, two months had come and gone. I was glad to be around them again. More than anybody, they understood what I was feeling. After all, what had been done to me had been done to them at one time or another, and our shared experiences equipped us with an understanding and perspective that was unfathomable to those around us. In truth, they were the only ones I could talk to, the only ones who could comprehend the complex jumble of thoughts and emotions that were constantly racing through my mind.

When I met back up with them, they were still in the local control unit that we were all moved to after the disturbance. I had returned to the scene of the crime, the place where the goon squad had tried in vain to take my life. Though my physical wounds had long healed, my ego was still bruised from the humiliation I had suffered after being dragged down the stairs and across the pod like a ragdoll.

They had moved us all to the bottom range by then to make it easier for the goon squad to enter our cells. We lived on constant alert, expecting an attack at any moment. In fact, not long after I returned to the pod, they rushed into Hasan's cell after he, once again, refused to take the annual tuberculosis test. As they had done with me, they saturated his cell with Mace before rushing in on him. I was but a few cells away and could hear the commotion. In protest, and out of a sense of solidarity, we all kicked on our cell doors and screamed obscenities. All of a sudden, Hasan came running out onto the range.

"Hell, yeah!" we all screamed in unison.

Though the goon squad was heavily armed, Hasan fought with them until, finally, they wrestled him to the ground and shot the serum into his arm.

"Get the fuck off of 'im, bitches!" we all yelled.

And then to further express our anger over what had occurred, we began setting off the sprinklers in our cells and flooding the range with water.

Every day was nonstop madness. For a time, in order to keep me out of the normal flow of things, I was forced to take my recreation on third shift, between midnight and two o'clock in the morning. I came out wearing two pairs of handcuffs and remained cuffed behind my back the entire time I was at recreation, which was nothing more than an empty cage—20 by 20 feet—situated in the center of the pod. This went on for several weeks until the administration saw how futile it was. Yes, I was handcuffed behind my back, but I was not muzzled. Hence, third shift or not, I gave them hell. I kicked and screamed until the rest of the pod (about 100 inmates) joined in on the ruckus. Before long, it was a full-blown demonstration.

"Ride me out," I told them whenever someone from the administration came around to monitor things. "'Til then, this is what it's gonna be." And I meant what I said. I had no intentions of stopping until I was transferred out-of-state.

Amid all this commotion, a rumor began circulating that the administration was building a special "uptight" pod for the five of us. It was hard to know whether or not this was true. But if it were, this special pod would no doubt be a torture chamber. Of that I was certain. Around the same time, there were articles in the newspaper about a new supermax facility being built in Youngstown, Ohio. Would we be sent there? It seemed unlikely since we were classified as death row and, according to the ARs, had to be housed in an area designated as such; this, despite the fact that we were currently being housed around inmates from the general population.

Time will tell, I thought. In the meantime, I hunkered down for another long winter in hell.

Death Row II

Drop everything if you find yourself in quicksand. Because your body is less dense, you can't fully sink unless you panic and struggle too much, unless you're weighed down by something heavy. Breathe deeply. Not only will deep breathing help you remain calm, it will also make you more buoyant. And remember: Take your time, as frantic movements will only hurt your cause. And whatever you do, do it slowly....[12]

From the very moment I received the indictment, I was filled with a sense of impending doom. I was unwilling to admit this to myself at first, but the mere thought of being executed filled me with great anxiety, a fear greater than that I had ever known. Here I had been innocently walking along, minding my own business, when all of a sudden I found myself buried waist-deep in quicksand. I panicked. In fact, everything I had done since being indicted and sentenced to death were the "frantic movements" of a man overcome with fear and dread.

Still, even as I felt myself going under, small windows of clarity opened up inside my mind and allowed me to see the futility in what I was doing.

Calm down, go slow, a voice inside of me cautioned. The more I tried to ignore this voice, the more insistent it became until, one day, I just decided to stop struggling and start listening more intently to its promptings.

You need some help, the voice inside me said. *You can't do it all alone.* But where would I find the help I needed? I did not know.

Several months prior to the disturbance in DR-4, I was on

---

[12] http://www.wikihow.com/Get-out-of-Quicksand

my way to the outside recreation area and met two people who, unbeknownst to me at the time, would become my greatest allies in the fight to save my life. They were meeting with George Skatzes after being introduced to his sister, Jackie Bowers, at a forum concerning the proposed opening of the supermax prison in Youngstown. They were sitting inside the conference room where inmates met with their attorneys and, just as I was about to walk by, George called out to me.

"Hey Keith!" he yelled, waving his hand excitedly in the air. "Come on in. I got two people in here I want you to meet."

This would not have customarily been allowed, but George sounded so enthusiastic in his request that I was permitted to walk into the room unimpeded. My hands were cuffed in front of me and I extended them as I moved forward. When the two strangers stood to greet me, I was instantly struck by how warm and kind they seemed. Indeed, their faces held the most compassionate smiles I had ever seen.

"Howdy!" I said, affecting a country accent to break the ice. "How y'all folks doin'?"

The gentleman, silver-haired and medium-built, laughed and extended his hand.

"Hi, I'm Staughton," he told me.

"And I'm Alice," the elderly woman standing next to him said, extending her hand in kind.

We exchanged pleasantries, but that was about it. Before I could ask any probing questions to find out who they were, the guard rushed me out the door.

"Nice to meet y'all," I called out over my shoulder.

I later learned from George that they were husband and wife and that they were retired Civil Rights attorneys. George did not let on just how heavily they had been involved in the Civil Rights Movement, or that Staughton was a famed historian and accomplished author of more than several books.

Not that any of this would have made a difference; by then, the quicksand had already risen to my chest and, though I took pains to camouflage the desperate state I was in, I felt it would only be a matter of time before I had to do something. Had I known who the Lynds were, and had I had more time to reveal to them what I was thinking and feeling, perhaps they could have thrown me the lifeline I so desperately needed. But we would meet again soon.

When the New Year arrived, rumors began to spread that we—the Lucasville Five—would be sent to the new supermax prison in Youngstown. Could this be true?

Again, I had my doubts. In the first place, I found it hard to believe that the administration would spend so much money to build a new isolation pod on the premises if they had no intentions on using it. Second, there was the matter of the ARs, which specifically stated: "All inmates sentenced to death under Ohio law... shall be assigned to an area of the institution... which shall be known as death row." A supermax did not fulfill that requirement.

Even with my doubts, however, I developed a sneaking suspicion that the rumors were more than mere speculation. After all, we were the alleged "leaders" of the uprising and the supposed reason why the supermax prison was being built in the first place; hence it made sense that we would be sent there and held up as the embodiment of the "worst of the worst."

"Oh, we're going," Jason, always the bearer of bad news, assured me again and again.

But when January, February, March, and then April came and went without any moves being made, I grew weary listening to the non-stop gossip. To guard against undue worry, I stood at a safe mental and emotional distance from it all, not totally unaffected by the rumors but convinced that whatever challenges lay ahead I would be able to face them with fortitude. Indeed, for the first time in a long time, I felt like I finally had my head on straight again. That being the case, it really did not matter where the next day found me. Supermax or not, I knew I was in for a long ride before I reached federal court, where things could be set right. In the meantime, I lived with everything I owned packed inside of a brown paper bag, ready to roll with the punches and absorb the "blows of fate."

In the early morning of May 7, 1998, I was startled out of a sound sleep by the blinding beam of a flashlight.

"What the fuck, man?" I demanded, instinctively raising my hand to shield my eyes from the glare.

"We need you to get up and get dressed, LaMar," someone said.

"I'm already dressed," I replied, rolling out of bed and turning on the cell light. I grabbed my face towel from the sink to wipe the sleep from my eyes. "What's up?"

The beam from the flashlight went dead. The face of a white man was staring through the window of the cell door. He seemed surprised to see that I already had my clothes on.

"You sleep in your clothes?" he asked, momentarily losing track of why he was there.

I looked at him and grimaced. I was not in the mood.

"We need you to pack up your belongings. We're moving you."

"I'm already packed," I told him, pointing to the paper bag on the side of the bed. I wrung the water from the towel and placed it inside. "Where am I going?" I asked, nonchalantly moving to an angle in the cell that allowed me to see out onto the range. The goon squad was standing there, waiting. I took a deep breath and moved toward the door. "Where am I going?" I inquired again.

"Turn around and cuff up."

When the cuffport opened, I hesitated, seized by a feeling of déjà vu.

"Turn around and cuff up, LaMar; I won't tell you again," he threatened, reaching for his Mace.

Reluctantly, I complied with the order and stuck my hands through the port. As soon as the cell door opened, three guards took hold of my arms and rushed me out the side entrance where four vans were waiting.

What is this? I wondered. My first suspicion was that I was being moved to the uptight pod, but obviously I was mistaken. *Oh, shit,* it suddenly dawned on me, *I'm going to the supermax!*

As I sat there, the realization of what was happening washed over me and I felt strangely at ease. *Finally,* I thought. I had lived through several months of the most intense pressure I had ever known, wondering and worrying about what would become of me, and now I knew. I took a deep breath and relaxed. I had come to the end of something very significant, and now I was moving on to the next phase of the journey.

I looked around at the guards, at the rising sun, moved back in my seat and smiled, convinced that whatever lay in front of me was nothing compared to what was now behind me. Even if my worst fears came true, nothing I encountered would ever be as difficult or painful as losing my grandparents, and I knew this with a certainty that made me feel invincible.

Don't even worry about it, I told myself, momentarily allowing my mind to race ahead.

Since there was more than one van, I assumed that I would not be the only one going, and I was right. I turned my head just in time to see Namir emerge from the building. They put him into the second van. Then came Hasan, followed shortly by Jason. They, too, were put into the second van.

Well, that leaves George, I thought to myself, guessing that he and I would be taking the ride together. But George never came out of the building.

That's strange, I said to myself, as the guard got into the van and started the engine. And then we were off, flying through the compound of the prison, through the gates, and up the interstate, headed east.

I hated riding in the back of the prison escort van. Nothing was more frightening than speeding down the highway in handcuffs and shackles, with no seatbelt on. If we got into a serious accident and the van somehow rolled over and caught on fire, I would surely die. In fact, I had read about just such an incident in the newspaper several weeks prior to being transferred and it terrified me to be in the exact same situation. The only thing I could do was grit my teeth and pray: *Please, God, don't let me die like this.*

In the front seat of the van, driving, was a member of the goon squad. He was in full riot gear, wearing the requisite aviator glasses. Next to him, in the passenger seat, was a lieutenant who sat stone-faced and silent, looking straight ahead. We were traveling in a four-van caravan: a lead van out front, two escort vans in the middle, and a tail van bringing up the rear. It was classic overkill, meant more to impress than anything.

But who are they trying to impress? I wondered. *Me? The citizens of Youngstown?* I had no idea.

When we arrived in Youngstown, a city that had fallen on hard times since the closing of most of its steel mills and factories, there was no one lining the streets to greet us. Indeed, we rolled through a ghost town filled with vacant houses and dilapidated buildings. The new prison would be a boon to the local economy.

As the van turned into the prison and began to make its way down the long driveway, I was struck by how pristine the grounds looked compared to the poverty-stricken area we had just driven through. According to newspaper reports, the new prison would cost taxpayers $65 million, and I could tell upon seeing it that this was probably true. It was state of the art.

No guard towers, I mumbled to myself, looking around somewhat unbelievingly. *Maybe I can escape,* I thought, momentarily allowing my mind to go on a flight of fancy. But who was I kidding? The fact that there were no guard towers meant that there was no means of escape, and on some level deep down inside I knew this. Still, in order to maintain a sense of hope, it is necessary to lie to oneself at times, and this was one of those times.

As the van pulled up to the sally port and came to a stop, the lieutenant reached for his walkie-talkie and barked orders into it. All of a sudden the doors on the vans flew open and the guards, shotguns drawn as if warding off an attack, jumped out and formed a protective barrier around the entrance. I turned around in my seat. It was a dazzling display.

Who are they trying to impress? I wondered. And then, out of the corner of my eye, I saw a videographer filming the whole thing.

This is crazy, I thought. *Twelve heavily-armed guards standing in the hot, scorching sun, wearing aviator glasses.* I shook my head. *They really believe this shit,* I mumbled to myself.

"LaMar, once we get you inside," the lieutenant said, cutting into my revelry, "I need you to remain calm; don't make any sudden movements." It was the first time he had spoken to me.

I nodded my head.

"We're gonna take you in and ask that you follow some very specific commands, okay?" he continued, in an urgent tone.

I nodded my head.

"We don't want to have to restrain you or anything..."

"What you mean, restrain me?" I asked, hearing a thinly-veiled threat in his warning. "What, y'all about to jump on me or something?"

"Oh, no, no, it's nothing like that. Just be cool and you'll be all right," he assured me.

I felt trapped.

"Yeah, okay," I told him, instinctively clenching my fists.

The gates opened and the van inched forward, moving into the prison proper. As we made our way through the second gate and around the winding road, I reminded myself to keep breathing. Then the van came to a stop in front of the garage door, which began to slowly open.

"Okay, this is it, LaMar!" the lieutenant announced as we pulled into the garage. "Remember what I told you: stay calm, keep your head straight, and don't make any sudden movements."

Beads of sweat were forming on my forehead. I was getting anxious, wondering if I was prepared to put into practice everything that I had learned.

I'm so tired of this shit, I said to myself, unclenching my fists. *Stay calm, keep your head straight, and no sudden movements*, I repeated, deciding to go with the flow. I could no longer allow my emotions to overrule my intellect. What had been done to me was finished and there was no turning back; the only way out was to move forward. *Be intelligent, Bomani,* a voice inside me said.

The van door opened and I scooted over in my seat,

readying myself to disembark. I took a glance out of the window: there were 30 or so guards lining the walkway leading into the building, each holding their PR-24 (night stick) in their hands. They looked menacing.

When my feet hit the ground, I began the long walk forward. With my head held straight, I made eye contact with each of the guards as I walked by. Never before had I seen such hatred and hostility; and yet, there was a weird quality to it all, as if it had been staged somehow. In fact, the footage being taken, I would later learn, would be used as a training tool for newly-hired guards.

"This is one of the most dangerous prisoners in the State of Ohio," trainees would be told. And there I was: 6'3", 220 lbs, looking every bit the part of the hardened criminal.

When I made it to the strip cage, I was told to remove my clothes. I complied, feeling a trickle of shame run down my spine as the female videographer paused the camera on my penis. I felt like an animal, like a non-person, a thing. It did not occur to me at the time, but this must have been similar to how newly arrived slaves felt when they disembarked from ships that delivered them into captivity. There was something inhumane in this procedure, something dirty, something unclean. But I went along with it. I had no choice.

"Lift your arms," the lieutenant ordered.

I obeyed.

"Open your mouth."

I complied.

Then I was told to turn around and show the soles of my feet.

"Okay," I whispered, feeling weak-kneed.

"Bend over. Spread your cheeks. Cough."

They were trying to emasculate me, to break my spirit by making me feel weak and powerless. I looked at the videographer when I turned back around: her hands were shaking; her face was red with embarrassment, proof that you cannot dehumanize someone without dehumanizing yourself in the process.

"Put on your clothes," the lieutenant instructed, pointing.

I looked to my left, and there, lying on the bench, folded into a neat stack, was a green prison uniform. *Where did that come from?* I wondered, noticing it for the first time since entering the room. I stepped into my underwear and pants, and then pulled on my shirt. I looked around for my socks.

"You won't be needing any socks here," the lieutenant told me, noticing the bewildered expression I had on my face. He had a thin, almost imperceptible smile on his lips. I slid my feet into the orange canvas shoes and sat down on the concrete bench. As I slowly came back to my senses, I noticed how cold it was in the room. I looked up at the air vent and folded my arms in front of me. A chill ran through my body. Presently, a big, 32-inch television was rolled in front of the glass door.

"Watch this!" the lieutenant barked, turning on the television and pressing the PLAY button on the VCR.

"My name is Warden Johnson," an elderly-looking white man announced, staring directly into the camera. It was hard to make out exactly what he was saying, but I caught bits and pieces of it.

"We will not tolerate any unruly behavior here at OSP," he said, sounding cold and indifferent. "You will follow the rules and regulations, or suffer the consequences!"

I had never heard a warden speak like this before. Typically those from the front office spoke more indirectly, but this was an outright threat. "If you get out of line, we are going to *deal* with you!" I got the message. And then, to follow up on what the warden had said, a local prosecutor named Paul Gains appeared on the screen:

"...then you will be prosecuted to the full extent of the

law.... We have at our disposal the means to bring you to justice...."

When the screen went dead, I looked up at the lieutenant and furrowed my brow, as if to say, *What now?*

I understood what was going on; this was the beginning of a long process to break me. A few months before I arrived at OSP, a manuscript was smuggled into the local control unit where we were being housed, and Jason passed it along to me.

"You gotta read this shit!" the note attached to the manuscript had said. I read it and was shocked by what I learned. At a conference in Washington, D.C., organized by the Federal Bureau of Prisons (BOP) in 1962, a psychologist by the name of Dr. Edgar H. Schein laid out the brainwashing methodology used for the "Breaking [of] Men's Minds."[13]

Of course it did not occur to me while I was reading it that I would soon be a "test subject" in the very same experiments that I was reading about. Nevertheless, something told me to take it seriously, and I did. I poured over the enumerated list that Dr. Schein provided to the group of administrators and wardens who had gathered to hear him speak. Apparently, the methods being put forth were to be implemented at the Federal Prison in Marion, Illinois, the forerunner of the supermax, where the stated goal was to "control revolutionary attitudes in the prison system...."

In his presentation, Dr. Schein spoke about the need to segregate those considered "natural leaders" and spelled out ways in which these individuals could be broken, including:

---

[13] Griffin, Eddie. "Breaking Men's Minds: Behavior Control in Human Experimentation at the Federal Prison in Marion." (Journal of Prisoners on Prisons, Vol. 4 No. 2, 1993).

- Prohibition of group activities not in line with brainwashing objectives.
- Segregation of all natural leaders.
- Spying on prisoners and reporting back private material.
- Tricking men into written statements which are then showed to others.
- Systematic withholding of mail.
- Disorganization of all group standards among prisoners.
- Building a group conviction among prisoners that they have been abandoned by and totally isolated from their social order.
- Undermining of all emotional supports.
- Convincing prisoners that they can trust no one.
- Preventing prisoners from writing home or to friends in the community regarding the conditions of their confinement.
- Making available and permitting access to only those publications and books that contain materials which are neutral to or supportive of the desired new attitudes.
- Placing individuals into new and ambiguous situations for which the standards are kept deliberately unclear and then putting pressure on him to conform to what is desired in order to win favor and a reprieve from the pressure....

The manuscript went on to speak about the constant clanging of the doors and the intentional rattling of the keys by the guards as a way to impinge upon the nervous system and thereby keep one in a constant state of agitation.

This is torture, I remember thinking to myself, shaking

my head in disgust. *Am I a natural leader?* I wondered aloud, pacing back and forth. *Is that what this is all about?*

I wrote Jason a note when I was done reading it:

"Is this shit real?" I asked, half-jokingly. "Wait, don't answer that: I already know."

And now, on my way out of the strip cell, I saw Jason across the clearing being led into a cell where he would undergo the same cycle of humiliation. Our eyes met as I walked past, and I gave him a wink of assurance. I was on my way to the cellblocks, and there was no way of knowing when, or if, I would see him again.

And where are Hasan and Namir? I wondered, unconsciously turning my head to look around.

"Keep your head straight!" one of the guards barked at me, tightening his grip on my arm.

"Oh, yeah, my bad," I apologized, a bit facetiously.

As we moved forward, I fought the instinct to peer to the left and right. I felt as if I was being led through a maze of some sort, up a corridor, down a corridor—and then we were standing in front of an elevator. I took a deep breath.

When the doors opened and I stepped inside, a guard pushed one of the buttons, setting the car in motion. A few seconds later we came to a sudden stop and my stomach lurched. The elevator doors opened up onto a small hallway: five short steps forward, a sharp turn to the right, and then we were standing in front of an electric door. One of the guards barked a code into his walkie-talkie and the door slowly opened. I took another deep breath and corrected my posture: shoulders back, chest out, eyes looking straight ahead.

When the way was clear, I took my first steps into B-block.

The Ohio State Penitentiary is made up of four cellblocks: A, B, C and D. Each block consists of eight pods (1-8) that contain 15 or 16 cells apiece for a total of 504 beds. How the State arrived at this arbitrary number is anyone's guess. But finding enough inmates who could be classified as the "worst of the worst" would prove virtually impossible and become the cause for much contention and legal wrangling as the State began to fill cells with those who did not meet the standards. Indeed, there was no standard, and when a lawsuit was eventually brought against them for violating inmates' right to due process, Jason and I would represent the inmate class. But this was a long way off yet.

Walking into B-block on that first day, I was filled with apprehension. The guards lined both sides of the hallway and stared icily at me as I walked by. I would be lying if I said it was not a little unnerving; it was. A guard had been killed during the Lucasville Uprising and more than likely they were told that I had something to do with it. What else could explain such blind hate?

We made our way around the control booth, which jutted out like the command center on a space ship, high in the air and set in a circular design that allowed the operator to see in a 360-degree radius.

The smell of fresh paint lingered in the air. Somewhere nearby I could hear the hiss of a welder's torch and the harsh-sounding ping of a hammer hitting metal. As we walked by pod 8, I saw a man up on a ladder painting.

Presently, we came to a stop in front of pod 5, and the door opened with a clamorous squeal:

Click-shhhhh-boom!

I would come to know this sound very well as the years dragged on; it would seep into my blood and bones and wreak havoc on my nervous system.

Entering the pod, the guards abruptly pushed me against the wall and demanded in a harsh tone that I lift my feet to allow them to remove the manacles from my ankles. I complied. And then they took off in a mad dash toward the back of the pod, carrying me with them. I thought they were going to run me headfirst into the wall, but they stopped short in front of cell 14. The door opened—*click-shhhhh-boom!*—and I was thrown inside like a piece of garbage. I was stunned.

What the fuck? I thought. The handcuffs were removed, the cuffport was slammed shut, and the guards turned and walked away without saying a word. I watched after them as they marched out of the pod, and never once did they break formation.

Mothafuckin' robots, I mumbled to myself.

I turned around and looked at my new surroundings. The cell was bigger than usual. It had the standard sink/toilet combination, a desk, a fixed stool, and a three-tier cabinet system on the wall. On the bed—a seven-foot slab of concrete with a razor thin mattress—were two sets of greens (i.e. prison uniforms), two pairs of underwear, two sheets, a blanket, a pillow and pillowcase, one bath towel, one face cloth, and an array of simple toiletries: liquid soap, toothpaste, deodorant, and so on.

I sat down on the bed and closed my eyes. I knew I was about to be put through hell, and I wondered if I had the "strength to go the length." I stood up and walked to the door, turned around and came back toward the bed; several hours passed in this way. I was thinking, organizing my thoughts and feelings. I stopped and looked at myself in the mirror.

Never allow yourself to be counted among the broken ones, I said to my reflection, remembering the words of George Jackson.

A guard came with a lunch tray and I refused it.

"I'm not hungry," I told him.

He looked at me with a bemused expression on his face.

"Suit yourself," he said, before speeding off down the range.

I made up the bed and got under the thin blanket. I was cold and tired. I fell asleep. Before long, another guard came with a dinner tray and, once again, I refused it.

"Don't want it," I told him.

He, too, looked perplexed.

"Are you on hunger strike or something?" he asked.

"Just not hungry, man," I told him, rolling over to face the wall.

I was exhausted; the last thing I wanted to do was eat. I wanted to sleep, to make the world disappear. I pulled the covers over my head and drifted off. I woke in the wee hours of the morning, shivering. It was so cold. *Damn!*

I got up and turned on the light and made my way to the toilet to relieve myself. Then I began my morning ablution: I washed the sleep out of my eyes and scrubbed under my arms, across my chest and torso.

Time to brush my teeth. When I searched for the toothbrush, I was shocked to discover that it was some kind of finger-brush that slid over the index finger and required me to stick nearly my whole hand into my mouth.

These mothafuckas are crazy, I mumbled to myself, squeezing the gel toothpaste onto the finger-brush. I was annoyed.

Though I felt a little faint from not eating, I moved to the center of the floor to begin my morning routine. I started with a few light stretches before performing my Sun Salutations, taught to me by my good friend, Da'im. Since it was so cold in the cell, I kept a brisk pace, moving from one pose to another, until beads of sweat appeared on my forehead. When I was sufficiently warmed up, I went into deeper poses, stretching my body while focusing on my breathing. Before I knew it, I was in a better state of mind, feeling composed.

When I was done with the yoga, I launched into an energetic round of calisthenics: jumping jacks, push-ups, sit-ups, and so on. When I looked up, the sun was peeking through the narrow window of the cell. I kneeled on the bed and looked out onto the manicured lawn, into the forest of trees beyond the perimeter fence. If I held my focus, I could almost convince myself that I was somewhere else, somewhere pleasant. But there was no time for such mind games. I went back to the sink and washed up again. Then I sat for my morning meditation. After about 30 minutes or so, a knock sounded on the door.

"Chow time," a guard announced, turning his key in the cuffport.

I opened my eyes and stared at him. I was sitting on my bed with my hands resting on my knees.

"Are you eating?" he asked, looking doubtful.

"Ain't no doubt," I told him, sounding more enthusiastic than I actually felt. I was surprised to see how much food was on the tray: pancakes, cereal, bacon and eggs, juice, milk and coffee.

Wow! I thought. *This might not be so bad after all.*

After breakfast, I slid back under the covers, chilled to the bone. I could not believe it was so cold, but this was exactly the kind of thing that Dr. Schein spoke about. With that in mind, I resolved not to complain and let my captors know that I was on to them.

Around eight o'clock or so, a group of administrators came around to speak with me. I was told that I would have to undergo a week of "orientation," which entailed reading a 30-page booklet that had been given to me. After the week was over, I would receive a television to participate in the "mandated programming" that had been specifically tailored to meet my "rehabilitation needs." The individual explaining all of this was the unit manager, a short, stalky white man with extremely tight civilian clothes. He had a short, square haircut consistent with someone who had served in the military or worked in law enforcement. And, to top it all off, his name was "Mr. Guard." I smiled when he introduced himself, thinking he had to be making up such a ridiculous name.

Yeah, right, I thought to myself, *and my name is Mr. Inmate. Nice to meet you.*

A few hours later I was offered recreation and I immediately jumped at the opportunity.

"Would you like to go inside or outside?" I was asked.

"Outside!" I exclaimed, thinking how nice it would be to feel the morning sun on my skin.

"Get ready, then," I was told. "We'll be back to get you in five minutes."

When they came back, I had all the things I needed to take a shower packed into a small tub that had been given to me. I was ready. I turned around to be cuffed, and when the door opened—*click-shhhhh-boom!*—I backed out slowly. The guards, who had been holding on to the handcuffs the entire time, immediately took hold of my arms and guided me in the direction they wanted me to move. Ten steps later, we came to a door marked, "Ex-A."

"Open Exercise A!" one of the guards barked into his walkie-talkie, and the door slowly opened. *Click-shhhhh-boom!* I was then shoved into a small room. The door closed behind me—*click-shhhhh-boom!*—and then the handcuffs were removed.

"Enjoy your recreation," one of the guards said, being sarcastic.

I was blown away. Outside recreation was a room with two four-foot long narrow slits cut into the wall; and the distinguishing feature that qualified the room as "outside recreation" was the fact that the slits had metal grating built into them with 100 or so holes drilled through them, letting in the occasional breeze.

I went and stood by one of the slits and looked outside.

I can't believe this shit, I said, shaking my head at the sheer absurdity of it.

"Is that you, Keith?" a familiar voice called out.

It was Jason.

"What's up, Jason!" I shouted, happy to hear his voice. "Can you believe this shit, man?" I said, more a statement than a question.

"These motherfuckers are crazy," he replied, laughing. "Did they come around and talk to you yet?" he wanted to know.

"Yeah, about eight o'clock or so."

"Did you meet Mr. *Guaaard*?" he asked, chuckling.

"That ain't that mothafucka's name, man!" I exclaimed, laughing for the first time in days.

"That's the same thing I said!"

We laughed and talked for about 10 minutes, comparing observations, making predictions—and then a voice came over the intercom and told us we were not allowed to talk to each other.

"Get the fuck out of here!" I heard Jason cry out in disbelief.

"Yeah, how the fuck y'all gonna tell us we can't talk?" I chimed in, pissed off at the mere suggestion that they thought they could tell us when and with whom to talk. Shortly thereafter, three guards appeared and told me that my recreation was over. They were each holding a can of Mace in their hands, ready to spray me if I showed the slightest signs of disobedience. No, I would not give them the satisfaction. As far as I could help it, I would never allow them to spray me, attack me, or degrade me ever again. I cuffed up and went back to the cell.

Sitting on the bed, I reflected on a time when, in order to prove a point, I would have defied their orders and forced them to do what they had been trained to do. And the point? To show them that I was a human being.

I had read Frantz Fanon's *The Wretched of the Earth* and had been moved to violence, believing it was the only way for me to express my humanity. But I had misunderstood. In the first place, I am not a country; I am a man, an individual with limited means and resources fighting against a system that is fully equipped to do me harm. Second, and most importantly, I came to understand that any acts of violence on my part would be used against me to prove and further substantiate the need to keep me isolated and subdued.

The guards came with their Mace, not because of what I had done (talk to another human being) but because they had been told I would overreact and blow things out of proportion. In that sense, they were responding, not to a man but to a profile, a profile that I had helped to create and was now expected to live up to.

But I had a trick for them. I would fight them, yes, but instead of using fists and knives, I would use my heart and mind to find my way forward. Would I be able to save my life? I did not know. But maybe, if I was earnest in my efforts, I could save some other young soul from having to suffer through the same ignorance and pain as I had. This was my only aim: to live in such a way that my life would not be in vain. I owed that to myself, to my grandfather, and to everybody who had taken the time to help me grow and see what my life could be.

I had already made a few feeble attempts to put my thoughts down on paper, but now I would dedicate myself to really learning how to write. I had heard it said, "The pen is mightier than the sword." Well, it was time to test that theory. I knew that the State had deprived me of a fair trial.

Furthermore, I understood that I could not expect the same system that betrayed me to turn around and save me. I had to save myself. But how? If I could not rely on the courts, who could I put my faith in—the people? Was there really such a thing as the "court of public opinion?" And if so, what would be their opinion of me, an admitted murderer? Would they deem me unworthy of justice? Would they say my life had no value?

There was only one way to find out, I reasoned. I had to tell my story. I had to lay it all out so people could get inside of it—feel it, live it—in order that they might begin to comprehend what it means to grope in darkness, to find a flicker of light, and then have that light snatched away just as they are beginning to ascend out of hell. Would I be able to do it? I did not know.

As anyone in my shoes would have felt, I experienced a definite sense of hopelessness from being isolated in such a way. The thought that I would never be able to go outside again hit me in the heart and made me feel sick to my stomach. Here I was in a pod by myself with no one to talk to, with no books to read; indeed, according to the orientation manual, we were not even allowed to have books, and the thought of that killed me. Books had been the one thing that had kept me from losing my mind. In fact, most of my "trusted friends" were the various authors I had been introduced to over the years of my incarceration: Richard Wright, Langston Hughes, Maya Angelou, Ralph Waldo Emerson, Kahlil Gibran, Claude McKay, Alice Walker, James Baldwin, Herman Hesse, George Jackson. These were my guides, the people on whom I relied to help me untangle the complexities of life, and now they were packed away inside of a box in the property room somewhere. I felt so alone....

When my week of orientation was up, I was given a black-and-white television. However, in keeping with the

Kafkaesque reality that was being fostered, the television came with no knobs attached to it, set to the institutional channel, preventing me from turning to a station of my choice. I laughed when I noticed it, but it was the laughter borne of desperation, not hilarity. There was nothing funny about what they were trying to do.

In the same week, George Skatzes, who had initially been left behind at ManCI, arrived at the supermax. A few weeks after his arrival, he received a visit from Alice and Staughton Lynd, the first-ever visitors to OSP. George and the Lynds were locked into opposite sides of a booth, separated by a glass partition, and George remained handcuffed behind his back the entire time. Staughton would later write that he left this initial visit with the desire "to tear OSP down." I shared a similar sentiment.

As more and more inmates began to arrive, it became evident that the "worst of the worst" was a purely relative term. Inmates who had racked up excessive conduct reports, who tested positive for drugs, or those with some kind of gang affiliation far outnumbered those with serious charges like rape, murder or aggravated assault. And mixed in with this haphazard collection of deviants were the mentally ill who, as one might imagine, suffered most from the harsh conditions.

Before long, as the true nature of the situation set in, each pod erupted in spontaneous pandemonium. For weeks on end, I had to stuff toilet paper inside my ears in order to blunt the constant yelling and banging on the doors. It was a mad house. The guards, not to be outdone, intentionally set off the fire alarms and then walked around with protective earmuffs to shield themselves from the piercing roar of the sirens, which blared night and day. It was exactly the kind of psychological warfare that Dr. Schein advocated. I was stupefied. Even though I had read about it, it was still hard to accept that they would deliberately try to torture us.

Is this really happening? I kept asking myself as each day rolled into the next.

And then, for no apparent reason, it stopped. The group of administrators came around and announced that, henceforth, we would be allowed to have newspapers, books and magazines, as well as sweat suits and various other miscellaneous items that had initially been denied: bars of soap, personal razors, socks, T-shirts, and so on. We were even given the knobs to the televisions! No one knew the cause behind this change of heart, but I was elated to know that we would be given our books.

I later learned what had happened: George and Hasan, along with nine other inmates who were housed alongside them in pod 1, went on a hunger strike and were able to enlist the help of Niki Schwartz, an attorney out of Cleveland, Ohio, who met with a Mr. Norm Hill, then north regional director of the Ohio Department of Rehabilitation and Correction, and convinced him to grant us additional property. In fact, Mr. Hill, along with Mr. Odell Wood, then deputy warden of operations at OSP, met personally with Hasan and went over the new property limits.

According to the new policy, we would be allowed four personal books beyond the one religious book and dictionary we were already entitled to. It was a small concession, but four books were better than no books.

I had over 50 books among my personal belongings in storage and was told that, with the exception of the four I was allowed to keep, the remainder would either have to be sent home, destroyed, or "donated" to the prison library. There was no way I was going to destroy my books; they meant too much to me. And since we were being forced to pay first class postage, I could not afford to send them home. Hence, through a kind of forced generosity, I bequeathed my beloved collection to the OSP library. And I was not the only one. Jason, who had the largest assortment of books of everybody, donated close to 100 volumes. In this way, OSP obtained one of the most prolifically diverse libraries in the Ohio prison system, with titles ranging from Adolf Hitler's *Mein Kampf* to Na'im Akbar's *Chains and Images of Psychological Slavery*.

Out of the 50 or so books I owned, I kept Viktor Frankl's *Man's Search for Meaning*; Richard Wright's *Black Boy*; Kahlil Gibran's *The Prophet*; and Shunryu Suzuki's *Zen Mind, Beginner's Mind*.

Man's Search for Meaning would give me the confidence of knowing that there was a way to get through the toughest of times with my heart and mind intact. "When you are confronted with circumstances you cannot change," advised Viktor Frankl, "the challenge is to change yourself." This I would try to do.

Reading *Black Boy* would teach me how to write, how to tell a story by capturing the essence of the experience. More than any author, Richard Wright's way of writing seemed the clearest, most forceful form of expression that I had encountered, and I would start each morning by randomly reading sections of his narrative in order to absorb the rhythm of his syntax.

The Prophet would nurture my soul and keep me from becoming too bitter about life. By contemplating the love and pain of life in Kahlil Gibran's poetic prose, I was able to develop in myself a more poetic approach to things, including God.

Zen Mind, Beginner's Mind would supply me with the framework to master my thoughts and emotions. I came to understand that it was my wayward emotions that had caused so much trouble in my life, and I was beginning to comprehend that they could be brought under control. The way to do that was through meditation and the practice of being mindful.

Years later, when restrictions loosened, I was able to read more books that delved deeper into the same themes, but I would never be without these four books. They were the glue that held things together in my life.

On August 13, 1998, the Fourth District Court of Appeals affirmed my convictions and death sentence. The news came as no surprise; I expected it. Three years had gone by since I had been sentenced to death and, according to what I had been told, it would be another 17 years before I could look for the relief I sought. Yes, it was a discouraging thought, but what could I do besides stay the course? In my panic-stricken, grief-ridden state, I had gone on two hunger strikes; I had initiated a major prison disturbance, after which I was beaten to within an inch of my life. I had been forced to sleep inside a mattress, to live out of a brown paper bag, and then sent to a supermax prison where it was certain I would undergo even more pain.

How would I survive? This was the question I asked myself. Seventeen years was an incredibly long time, too long. So I broke it down; instead of years, I would think in terms of months; and if a month felt too long, I would break it down even further to weeks, sometimes days—minutes if need be. I would focus only on what I knew I could do, nothing more; for the goal was not merely to survive another 17 years, but to survive it with my heart and mind intact. How would I be able to do that?

By the time I arrived at OSP, I had already made the shift in my mentality that allowed me to see things more clearly. I knew how to protect myself now. Each morning, and several times throughout the day, I closed my eyes and meditated. In the beginning, while I was still at Mansfield, I started out with an easy routine (again, taught to me by my friend, Da'im) of counting my breaths—each inhalation and exhalation equaling one—until I got to 10. And then I started over. The only rule to this seemingly simple exercise was that if I lost my count I had to begin anew.

At first, I could barely make it through one complete rotation without losing my count, but with steady practice I was able to strengthen my focus. When I could consistently count 100 uninterrupted breaths, I stopped counting and concentrated solely on my breathing. In this very uncomplicated way, I taught myself how to meditate. It was the key to my salvation.

"When you are practicing Zazen," advised Shunryu Suzuki, "do not try to stop your thinking. Let it stop by itself. If something comes into your mind, let it come in and let it go out. It will not stay long."

By learning how to watch my thoughts, I was able to rise above the vicious cycle of cause and effect, and thereby avoid the tricks and traps of my environment. Indeed, I was living in a twisted world, a place where those in authority believed it was their "job" to push individuals over the edge. Hence, it was nothing to leave the cell and come back to find one's personal property—pictures, envelopes, stationery—scattered all over the cell floor or, worse, thrown into the toilet.

In fact, I came back from recreation one day and found my grandmother's photo floating in the commode (cause). Tell me, how was I supposed to react to this? Get upset (effect)? Then what? Should I have kicked on the door and screamed obscenities at the guards whom I suspected of disrespecting my possessions? Had I done any of these things, I would have opened myself up to an attack. But I was hip to the game and managed to remain calm. After all, my grandmother was not an image on a piece of paper, but someone who lived deep within the private chambers of my heart.

It was my grandmother who had taught me the story of Job in the Bible. She told me how Satan had come to God and asked permission to tempt Job, God's most faithful servant, and how God had granted Satan his wish, with the condition that Satan was not allowed to touch Job. When she finished telling me the story, which was recounted all from memory, she looked at me with a serious expression on her face.

"Never forget that, Keith," she said. "If you keep your faith in God, Satan cannot touch you." Sitting alone in my cell now, I remembered this.

Every day there was a new round of madness: screaming, banging, beatings, shootings, cell extractions. It never ceased. Soon, unable to endure the constant pressure, a few men tried to kill themselves but were ultimately unsuccessful. Then, in February 1999, an inmate carried it all the way through. For those of us who were not in the pod with him, word of his death reached us through the guards. They spoke about it as though it was something positive, as if the inmate had done something worth repeating.

"He sure knew what he was doing!" they said.

After the second suicide in July 1999, someone from the administration contacted Alice and Staughton, asking them to intervene. Alice then sent a form letter to 100 OSP inmates in which she posed the question: "If someone asked you, WHAT COULD OSP DO TO MAKE YOU FEEL YOUR LIFE IS MORE WORTH LIVING, what would you say?"

I received one of the letters.

I had not seen the Lynds since being introduced to them by George Skatzes in the attorney/client room at Mansfield. A lot had happened since that time and I was not sure how they felt about me. By now I had turned around and was no longer dedicated to a path of self-destruction. I wanted to share what I had learned from my mistakes with those who were now suffering through the same fear and confusion that had nearly driven me over the edge. I wrote Mrs. Lynd a letter:

20 July '99
Dear Mrs. Lynd:

If someone asks me, "What could OSP do to make me feel my life is more worth living," I would say:

I don't know that anything material can be applied that would make me feel my life is more worth living. Every day I wake up with the knowledge that, at some point during the day, I'm going to be humiliated and that this little space in which I exist is going to be violated; and that whatever attempts I make toward maintaining my humanity will be challenged by an attitude of indifference that's designed to make me feel like an animal. And I would say: it doesn't matter if you gave me all the televisions and commissary in the world; none of these "things" will make a difference if the willingness isn't there to treat me like a human being.

I could have stopped there, because a shift in perspective was fundamental to any sincere attempt to remedy what was going on. The administration had to be willing to acknowledge our humanity before they could begin to treat us like human beings. But I knew that they were only trying to put forth a positive front in order to stave off negative publicity. So I continued, directing my comments at those who might read what I was thinking and feeling:

Indeed, if I thought the administration was truly concerned with the quality of our lives, I would be the first to make suggestions. However, we all understand by now that this is all about money (plain and simple) and that the quality of our lives isn't nearly as important as the quantity of dollars that this money machine is designed to make. Personally, I think guys need to look within themselves for the validation of their worth, because as far as I am concerned, no one can make you feel worthy if you don't first recognize your own value as an individual....

We have to look within and prepare a place there in which we can retreat and be ourselves. And this may require that we learn how to be still and listen to what's going on within.... Meditate, work out, and keep a journal—that's how you make it through the day. And take one day at a time. Stretch before you go to sleep....

* * * * *

I never found out what the result of this inquiry was, but if the administration instituted any "preventive measures" to quell the tide of suicides, I failed to see any proof of it. In fact, in April 2000, another inmate took his life.

It was hard being surrounded by so much pain. But I knew how they felt. I had felt the same way. The only difference is that, in my pain, I discovered that there was something indestructible inside of me; and more than that, that this something was highly intelligent and able to assist me in my struggle to overcome what I was going through.

During a moment of clarity, surrounded by pain on all sides, I grabbed my journal and wrote the following lines:

God is alive and
resides inside of us.
All we have to do is trust
and have faith,
stop the madness and give thanks
for the blessings that shape our lives....
We have to look ahead instead
of always looking back at the past,
slow down instead of moving so fast,
and laugh, reach deep and have
the courage to dream
about beautiful days
and different ways
to give, with love...in peace.

Death Row III

On May 15, 2002, the Supreme Court of Ohio affirmed my convictions and death sentences. On hearing the news, I shrugged my shoulders. With respect to whether or not my constitutional rights were violated when exculpatory evidence had been withheld during my trial, the justices voted unanimously that the "hide the ball" game played by the trial court and the prosecution did not constitute a *Brady* violation. Although I had been warned that this would happen, I was still a bit disappointed.

In an effort to educate myself on the issue, I had read a plethora of court pleadings that revolved around the suppression of exculpatory evidence—*Burger v. United States, United States v. Bagley, United States v. Agurs, Giglio v. United States, Napue v. Illinois*—and what occurred in my case seemed far more "egregious" than anything I had encountered in my perusal of these benchmark cases. But I was moving on, and that was the important thing.

Shortly after my case was finalized in state court, I was appointed two new attorneys named Kate McGarry and Angela Miller who, in keeping with the custom, were recommended by the attorneys who had represented me on direct appeal, who, in turn, had been recommended by my trial attorneys. It was not exactly what I would call a science, but, without the funds to shop around, I consented to it. "You're in good hands," I was invariably told.

When I met with Kate and Angela for the first time, I was impressed by how forthright they were. Most attorneys are experts when it comes to double-speak, but they seemed sincere and intent on telling me the truth.

"This is a highly political case," they admitted, looking serious, "and it's going to be an uphill battle...."

The use of the word "battle" let me know that they were

prepared to fight, and I felt encouraged by that. The only real drawback centered on the fact that Kate lived in New Mexico.

"Isn't that kind of far away?" I ventured, looking doubtful.

"Yes, it is," she admitted, "but you'll be seeing a lot of me, I promise."

And for the most part she would hold true to her word, coming to see me at least 3-4 times a year in the ensuing years, which was more than Mrs. Miller who lived in Ohio. Indeed, it was with Kate that I would eventually establish the better rapport. I appreciated her no-nonsense attitude and mental toughness. I was also impressed by her legal acumen; she seemed to know a lot about the law. But even more important than that, I got the sense that she was not the kind of person who would allow herself to be compromised or put into a position that would leave me in the lurch.

As I moved deeper into the process, I somehow got the feeling that it would come down to whether or not my attorneys "kept it real." For some reason, I could not bring myself to believe that the federal courts would rubberstamp what had been done to me; however, in order to receive the relief I sought, the issues would have to be properly presented and argued, and I felt I could trust in Kate to do that.

As I had done with all my lead attorneys, I sent her a photo of me to serve as a reminder that I was a real person and not just a name on a piece of paper. I felt it was important that she understood this and not forget it. On visits, after we were done talking about legal matters, I talked to her about my life, about my troubled childhood, and about how difficult it had been for me to overcome the dysfunction that I was born into. I told her of my dreams and aspirations, which revolve around helping "at-risk" youth by sharing with them the knowledge of my experiences. And she told me about her own life and some of the hurdles that she had overcome.

"So, okay," I said to her one day, "here we are, two human beings standing at the crossroads, and I need your help, Kate. I need you to help me fight for my life."

"I'll do my best, Keith," she told me, nodding her head.

"That's all I expect you to do. And maybe your best won't be good enough," I said, thinking about the 'uphill battle' in front of us. "But that's alright. We won't worry about that right now. Just please don't sell me out, Kate."

"I'm not going to sell you out, Keith," she assured me, smiling, shocked that I would suggest such a thing.

But I was not smiling. I wanted her to understand that I was not going to sit idly by and allow myself to be "screwed."

"I'm not going out like that, Kate," I told her.

"Well, I'm not going to sell you out, Keith."

I looked into her eyes and nodded my head.

"Okay," I said. "But, tell me, what would you do if you were in my shoes?"

"What do you mean?"

"I mean, if you were on death row for something you didn't do and they were trying to kill you, what would you do?"

"Well, I would try to tell as many people as possible about my case and see if I could generate some support—that's what I would do."

"That's exactly what I intend to do, Kate," I told her. "I'm not going to spend my time hounding you, writing and calling you every day to see if you are doing your job; I'm not going to do that. I'm going to read everything you file, and if I have any questions, I'll write or call you, okay?"

"That sounds fine to me, Keith," she said.

And so that was our agreement: I would leave her alone

to concentrate on my case and, to the extent that I could, try to generate some support on my own. Having established this understanding, things went smoothly for a while. And then things went terribly wrong.

On August 16, 2004, Kate and Angela filed my habeas corpus petition. Shortly thereafter, the State filed a motion to dismiss on statute of limitations grounds, claiming that my petition had been filed nine months too late.

I was flabbergasted when I heard the news. We had barely gotten underway and already the State was trying to have me killed without hearing my 25 claims for relief (See Appendix I).

"What's this all about, Kate?" I asked when she came to see me.

"Well, calm down and I'll explain it," she told me.

"I'm calm!" I lied, anxious to hear what she had to say.

"Okay, when your case was finalized in state court in December of 2002," she began slowly, "we had a year from that time to file your habeas petition, which means it was due in December of 2003—"

"Right, right," I interjected, letting her know I was following along.

"Well, instead of filing the petition in December, we elected to file a 26B motion."

"You mean that 'ineffective assistance of appellate counsel motion,' right?" I asked, remembering.

"That's right. Well, based on the controlling law at the moment [*Bronaugh v. Ohio*], the 26B motion is considered part of your direct appeal and tolls the statute of limitations."

"What do you mean by, 'tolls the statute of limitations'?" I asked, a little confused.

"It stops the clock, in other words," she told me.

"Yeah, yeah, I remember you explaining that to me before," I said, relaxing. "So what's the big deal then?" I asked, bewildered. "I don't get it."

"Yeah, well, the State is arguing that the 26B motion is part of collateral review and does not toll the time. In fact, there's a case [*Pace v. DiGuglielmo*] being litigated right now that will determine whether or not that's true," she told me.

"Oh," I muttered under my breath, seized by a sudden flash of clarity. "But what does that have to do with me?" I wondered aloud.

"We'll see, Keith."

I could not believe that the courts would actually consider throwing my case out based on a law that was not even in effect yet. And to make matters worse, my co-counsel, Angela Miller, abruptly withdrew from the case without an explanation.

"What happened?" I asked Kate when she delivered the news.

"I don't really know, to be honest."

"You mean she didn't give you an explanation or nothing? She just up and quit?" I asked, dumbfounded. Something was not right.

"I don't know what happened, Keith," she intoned, shaking her head. "But listen, I have the names of two attorneys who are ready to replace her; you can pick either one," she said, closing the door on my inquiry into Mrs. Miller's disappearance.

"Which one of them is the best?" I asked, flustered.

"They're both pretty good," she said, noncommittally.

I felt uneasy, as if I was being asked to pick a name out of a hat or something. I squirmed in my seat.

"And I gotta pick right now?" I asked.

"Well, yeah, we have a lot going on and I can't do it all by myself."

"I know, I know," I said, nodding my head in understanding.

I forget the name of the first attorney, but I had heard of David Doughten, the second suggestion, and decided on the spot to go with him.

A few weeks later, I was still a nervous wreck, worrying about whether or not my case would be thrown out. When I talked it over with Staughton, he seemed convinced that I was overreacting.

"I wouldn't worry about it if I were you," he told me, waving his hand as if to dismiss the matter outright. "Just keep working on your manuscript," he said.

By then I had already completed the first edition of *Condemned*, a small booklet detailing the bare bones of my ordeal, and had begun writing my autobiography, *Straight Ahead*.[14] However, I would be lying if I said my thoughts were not hampered by the weight of the impending court decision. I paced the floor incessantly, unable to sleep.

And then, several months later, in April of 2005, the court decided in *Pace v. DiGuglielmo* that a 26B motion was part of collateral review and *did not* toll the statute of limitations. Hence, the final recommendation by Judge Michael Merz, the magistrate judge presiding over my habeas petition, was that "Statutory tolling was precluded by the new law," but added: "Petitioner may have an opportunity to show that he is entitled to an evidentiary hearing on equitable tolling." I was astonished. *They're really trying to throw out my case*, I thought.

When it came down to it, though, Staughton was right—there was no need to worry.

On June 21, 2006, District Judge Thomas Rose entered the final order on the issue:

---

[14] At the completion of this manuscript, my autobiography, *Straight Ahead*, has not yet been published.

Pursuant to federal retroactivity juris-prudence, LaMar's Ohio rule 26B application is a direct appeal. As such, and in accordance with *Bronaugh*, it tolls the statute of limitations. LaMar is entitled to statutory tolling. LaMar's Objections to Judge Merz' Supplemental Report and Recommendation regarding Statutory tolling are GRANTED.

Finally, following the de Nova review required by 28 U.S.C. and 636(b) and Federal Rules of Civil Procedure Rule 72(b), the Court adopts Judge Merz' Supplemental Report and Recommendation as it applies to Equitable Tolling in its entirety. The Warden's objections to the Supplemental Report and Recommendations are OVERRULED. LaMar is entitled to an evidentiary hearing on the issue of Equitable Tolling.

Finally, after years of being dismissed and blatantly disrespected, I heard the word "granted" in relation to something that was in my favor. True, I had not yet received the relief I sought, but, as I was made to understand, an evidentiary hearing was a rare and momentous thing. I would now be allowed to question the very people who had deprived me of a fair trial; now it was their turn to take the stand and explain their actions. I was ecstatic.

The evidentiary hearing was set for July 8-9, 2007, at the federal courthouse in Dayton, Ohio. In the month leading up to the occasion, I put the call out to my family and friends to converge on the courthouse en masse. If ever I needed the love of my circle, it was now. I needed them to be my "witnesses," to hear and see for themselves what had been done to me.

A week before things were set to get under way, I was

moved to the Lebanon Correctional Institution in Lebanon, Ohio. Given that it was only 15 minutes away from Dayton, it was decided that it would be easier—and safer—to transport me back and forth to the courthouse from there.

I had begun my prison term at Lebanon in 1989 when I was 19 years old. In fact, it was at Lebanon that I first learned how to box. It was also there, while searching through the dusty African-American section of the library, that I discovered Malcolm X and began the journey to reclaim my life. And now, almost 18 years later, I was returning.

Walking into the prison on that humid July morning, I was surprised to see that the hallways had been cleared to meet my arrival. As I made my way down the corridor, curious onlookers peered from behind closed doors. *Here comes the bad guy again*, I thought to myself, as I was led to the L-1 hole, a sweltering part of the prison where inmates are sent to be punished.

As soon as I walked through the door, the heat hit me in the face like a wall of fire, causing beads of sweat to instantly form on my forehead. I looked around like a trapped animal. In a corner, off to the side, a rickety old fan whirled, circulating the dank and musty air around the dimly lit pod. I took a deep breath. I would be locked in a "high-security" cell on the second range, I was told. I nodded my head. *This is how it always is*, I thought. No matter where I went, I always found myself restrained or cooped up in a cage like a madman. It was a demoralizing thought, but I let it come in, and then let it go out of my mind. There was no time to dwell on the negative. I had to stay focused.

On the morning of August 8, the day of the hearing, I woke early and went over my legal briefs for the hundredth time. I was anxious. The issue of equitable tolling was important, but I had already been granted statutory tolling, which meant my habeas petition had been filed on time after all. My focus was now centered on whether or not the judge would agree that my constitutional rights were violated when the State withheld exculpatory evidence during my trial.

When I arrived at the courthouse, I was escorted to a holding cell that was adjacent to the courtroom. It was thereupon explained to me that before I would be allowed to enter, I would have to sign a "waiver" giving my consent to have an electro-shock bracelet placed around my ankle.

I looked at the agent with a quizzical expression on my face. It sounded like he was asking me to wear a device that was designed to electrocute me, but my mind was slow to accept this as a true statement.

"I don't understand," I said.

The agent, a white man in his late fifties, held up what appeared to be an ankle weight: it was black with Velcro straps attached.

"If you cause a disturbance or try to escape," he told me, somewhat nonchalantly, "this will send an electric current through your body and disable you."

I raised an eyebrow when he said that.

"What! Why would I agree to wear some crazy shit like that?" I asked, with a frown on my face.

"Well, you either wear the bracelet or I'll put you in full restraints," he told me, unperturbed. "It's your choice."

There go those words again, I thought. It was always my choice: take a deal or die? Lethal injection or the electric chair? Electro-shock or full restraints? My whole life, it seemed, was nothing more than a long train of false choices, of being forced to choose between the lesser of two evils. And the truly sad thing is that I had grown accustomed to it. Sitting there, I thought about my five-year-old niece, Kayla, who would be in attendance. The last thing I wanted to do was frighten her.

"You got an ink pen?" I asked, with a sigh of resignation.

After surrendering my signature, the agent wrapped the bracelet around my ankle and fastened it. He then adjusted my pant leg and concealed it from view. *Well, that's not too bad*, I thought, looking down at my leg.

When it was time for things to get underway, I took a deep breath and tried to steady my nerves. I had gone through a lot to arrive at this place in the process and was hoping to find that it had not all been in vain. *Will my family and friends show up?* They were traveling from all over the state, and I worried that not all of them would be able to make the journey. But when I walked through the courtroom doors, I was greeted by the most beautiful sight I had ever seen. Everybody was there.

Alice and Staughton were there. My mother, aunts and uncles were there; and standing in the midst of them all was my little niece, Kayla, with her backpack on. I smiled and waved when I saw her, happy in the secret knowledge that I had spared her the sight of seeing me in handcuffs and shackles.

I looked around the courtroom at all the people who had come out to lend their support, stopping at each individual to acknowledge their presence. "Thank you... Thanks... Nice to see you..."

Sitting in the front row was my comrade, Kunta Kenyatta. More than anybody, he knew what I had endured and suffered. He had been at Lucasville when Operation Shakedown was implemented and had been put through the same insanity as the rest of us. As fate would have it, however, he was in the hole when the uprising jumped off, and now, finally, after spending a few years at the supermax, he had made it home. I balled up my fist and touched the left side of my chest. "I love you, brah," I mouthed.

He nodded his head. Yes, he understood the magnitude of the moment.

Presently, the bailiff called for order in the court and the Honorable Judge Merz—short, rotund, and cloaked in black robes—made his way to the bench. I watched as he settled onto his perch. He had a kind face, almost cherublike. He picked up a pen and began to write something down on a piece of paper. Next, he leaned to his right and mumbled something to the stenographer, and then shot a furtive glance in my direction before surveying the scene. Satisfied that everything was in order, he allowed the proceedings to commence.

Consideration of the *Brady* issue began by calling Special Prosecutor Mark Piepmeier to the stand. He was the one who had created the criteria by which the wheels of (in)justice had been set in motion. By now, I had heard his name uttered a million times and had imagined him to be a cloven-hoofed creature with shifty eyes and a tail. Instead, he looked just like the average attorney: bespectacled, studious, and alert. Looking at him, at his cool and calm demeanor, I had to remind myself that the devil was not in his appearance but in the details of what had been divulged.

In the deposition leading up to the evidentiary hearing, Mr. Piepmeier disclosed that the State had used what would later be termed a "narrow *Brady* standard" when it came to determining what evidence to turn over to the defense. For example, he testified that "because so many assaults during the riot were committed by more than one person, the fact that a witness testified that 'inmate X committed an assault for which inmate Y' was charged [it] was not considered to be exculpatory as to inmate Y unless the witness specifically excluded inmate Y as an assailant."

It was an odd formulation, but it explained why a statement made by an inmate named Michael Jones ("witness"), who claimed to have seen an inmate named Frederick Frakes ("inmate X") kill William Svette—an inmate that I ("inmate Y") was found guilty of murdering—was never turned over. Since Michael did not "specifically exclude [me] as an assailant," his statement was not considered exculpatory.

Now on the stand, Mr. Piepmeier went on to explain his bizarre application of *Brady*:

> Let's say... there were 11 inmates in there beating on Svette. Half of them were masked, half of them weren't. And of the half that weren't I knew the one and his name was... inmate Powers. I would not see that as exculpatory to inmate LaMar.

This was not a hypothetical scenario. In fact, an inmate named Belcher, whose statement was before the court as exhibit 13, claimed to have witnessed an inmate named Powers drop a weight on the head of William Svette. And nowhere in his statement did he mention my name. According to Mr. Piepmeier, the statement was not exculpatory because "there could be another form that Belcher identified LaMar doing something." But there was no such form, at least not one that was ever produced.

I looked around the courtroom to see if those in attendance were paying attention; most of them were shaking their heads in disbelief.

And then came Prosecutor Seth Tieger to the stand. It had been 12 years since we had last seen each other. A feeling akin to hate rose up in me as I watched him take his seat. He still had the same smug expression on his face. Like Mr. Piepmeier, Prosecutor Tieger did not consider Belcher's statement exculpatory because "a number of different inmates assaulted [Svette] in different places." He was then asked about an inmate named Sam Batson— whose statement was before the court as exhibit 15—who identified Anthony Walker, a key witness for the prosecution, as the actual killer of Albert Staiano, one of the inmates for whom I had been sentenced to death.

"Let me ask you," my attorney said, standing up at the defense table, "if there were statements that were inconsistent with what your witnesses were saying, would you deem those to be exculpatory?"

It was a loaded question: if he answered yes, it would mean he knowingly and willfully deprived me of a fair trial; if he answered no, it meant he never intended to give me a fair trial in the first place. Sensing the significance of the moment, my family and friends leaned forward in their seats.

Prosecutor Tieger began to fidget. *Is that a crack in his armor? Answer the question.* He turned to face the audience and threw his head back in a defiant manner.

"Not necessarily," he responded, looking down his nose at us.

There was an audible gasp among the spectators. I looked at my mother; she had tears in her eyes. I took a deep breath and exhaled slowly, glancing down at my pant leg.

When Prosecutor Tieger got up from the stand and made his way from the courtroom, he walked past me as if I was invisible, as if he could not see me sitting there. And this, too, was a willful act: in order not to acknowledge my presence, he had to keep his head perfectly straight and his eyes fixed in a forward position. No matter what, he could not allow himself to recognize my humanity. Had he done that, he would have had to admit that what he did to me was wrong, and he could not bring himself to do that. After all, I was a criminal and, as far as he was concerned, had forfeited my claims to justice.

Next, Prosecutor Bill Anderson, who had served as co-counsel alongside Prosecutor Tieger during my trial, took the stand and spoke to the very dicey dilemma that they had been in: "We were trying to protect ourselves from being the ones that made the call on what was exculpatory and what wasn't," he said.

Question: Why would they need to protect themselves from being "the ones" to provide me with a fair trial when it was their duty under the Constitution to do exactly that? But, should we not speak honestly about these things? Had Prosecutors Tieger and Anderson followed the law, the jury would have heard all the conflicting evidence that, more than likely, would have changed the outcome of my trial.

For instance, had the jury been able to hear Sam Batson's testimony, he would have testified that it was Anthony Walker, one of the State's key witnesses against me, who killed Albert Staiano. Is it not reasonable to assume that their judgment would have been affected by this knowledge? Or, say, the jury would have heard Michael Jones' testimony, who would have testified that it was Freddie Frakes, not me, who killed William Svette. Would this not have made a difference? What about Aaron Jefferson's confession, wherein he admitted to killing Darrell Depina? Should not the jury have heard this evidence? Indeed, had this evidence been turned over, there is a "reasonable probability" that its use would have resulted in my acquittal.

When Prosecutor Anderson left the stand, Judge Merz called for a recess. The mood inside the courtroom was tense. After hearing the prosecutors all but admit that they had deprived me of a fair trial, my family and friends were visibly upset. Judge Merz, no doubt sensing the dissatisfaction among the spectators, rushed to reassure them that he was tuned in. "It's really nice to see so many people in attendance," he said, with an empathetic expression on his face. "These are very important cases...."

Later, during the same break, he crossed paths with

Alice and Staughton in the hallway and informed them that he was familiar with "their work," apparently alluding to the book Staughton had written about the disturbance (*Lucasville: The Untold Story of a Prison Uprising*). Staughton mentioned this to me afterward and said, "Maybe this guy has an open mind."

And so the evidentiary hearing ended on a relatively high note. We had forced the State to admit that they had used a "narrow standard" to determine what constituted exculpatory evidence. Now, having heard their testimony, the process demanded that Judge Merz take the matter under advisement, after which he would issue a report and recommendation as to what he deemed should be done with my case.

"How long will that take?" I asked my attorneys.

"Well, it's hard to say," I was told. "Sometimes these things can take between one and two years. Sometimes longer...."

This is how it is if you get caught in the web of the criminal justice system: it takes very little time to get stuck, but years and years to untangle yourself.

I was riding on a high when I made it back to OSP, and then I sank into a deep depression. Being surrounded by my family and friends gave me a definite sense of just how isolated I had been, and now that I was back inside the "tomb" I felt doubly disconnected and alone. Fourteen years had come and gone since the Lucasville Uprising and I still had not been afforded the opportunity to hug or hold my loved ones, a fact that was slowly eating away at my resolve. *There's gotta be something I can do*, I kept telling myself. *But what?*

Not long after I had returned, Staughton sent me a book entitled *Nothing But An Unfinished Song* by Denis O'Hearn. When I received it, I opened it and read it straight through. It was about an Irish prisoner named Bobby Sands who, along with several of his comrades, died while on hunger strike. They were protesting against the British government's insistence on classifying them as "criminals" when, as far as they were concerned, they were enemy combatants and should be treated as "prisoners of war" and accorded the deference delineated by the Geneva Convention.

I was instantly captivated by the sense of agency involved in their struggle. Instead of blindly accepting the definitions foisted upon them by those in power, they—under the banner of the IRA—set out to define life according to their own vision and values.

Although from totally different backgrounds and upbringings, I saw a lot of the same patterns in Bobby's development that I had undergone (and in some ways, was still undergoing). There was something almost prescient about his story and the tragic way in which it ended. It felt as if I was reading about my own life in some way. As I poured over the pages, I caught an abiding sense that I was being sent a message. In years past, whenever I found myself plagued by doubt and confusion, something (or someone) would show up to point the way forward—and most times these messages came in the form of books. In time, I came to view these occurrences as more than mere coincidences, but as "answers" to the various questions I projected out into the universe. "What can I do to put myself in a position to be able to hug and hold my family again?" I had asked. And the universe responded.

A hunger strike? Just the thought of starving myself again caused me to shake my head. *No, I'm not going through that again,* I said to myself, remembering. After reading the book a second time, I decided that I needed to reach out to the author. If nothing else, I wanted to let him know that his book had found a receptive soul, and that the toil of his task had not been in vain.

I wrote Staughton and, after explaining how much I had been affected by the book, asked if there was some way he could forward a letter to Mr. O'Hearn for me.

"Write the letter and send it to me; I'll make sure he gets it," he responded.

So I did. I sat down at my typewriter and poured out my heart:

10 November 2007
Dear Mr. O'Hearn:

My name is Keith LaMar (aka Bomani Shakur), and I am one of the five men who was sentenced to death following the Lucasville Prison Uprising in 1993. A few months ago, Staughton Lynd, who is a good friend of mine, arranged to have your fine book sent in to us—"The Lucasville Five"—and I'm writing to commend you on writing such a powerful piece. Existing as I do in the belly of the beast (so to speak), it's not often that I get the opportunity to use the word "beautiful," but your book is that and more. I truly enjoyed it.

According to Edmund Wilson, author of *To the Finland Station,* "The importance of a book depends, not merely on the breadth of the view and the amount of information that has gone into it, but on the depths from which it has been drawn." Using this as my yardstick, I have to say that your book is perhaps the most important book that I have ever read. And I say this because, out of all the books I've read, yours has gone the farthest in helping me understand some of the deeper elements of what I have been involved in. Indeed, as improbable as it may sound, Bobby and I have traveled along some of the same paths to some of the same conclusions, and I think you are right when you say that he was "forced into a new identity." I feel the same way about myself, although I've never really looked at it in that way before. To a large extent, I think we (and when I say "we," I'm wondering if you'll agree with me?) are cultivated from a very early age to play very specific roles, and that it is only through the process of providence that we become that which we were meant to be: human beings. To be sure, not everyone answers the call, but for those of us that do, life becomes imbued with meaning.

When I came to prison 19 years ago, I was 19 years old, which means I have been here for exactly half of my life. When I came here, I had absolutely no awareness of the forces that created me, nor the context into which I was born; as far as I was concerned, I was just another "dumb nigger" who was destined to live out his life in darkness. However, like Bobby, I met and was mentored by some very remarkable men who gave me a different take on life; and through these men, these angels, I've been able to reestablish and assert a more authentic identity. Of course, this has led me to my present predicament (ironically), but, speaking honestly, I wouldn't have it any other way. Here, in the "fell clutch of circumstance," I have discovered something much more purposeful to commit my life to and, again, like Bobby, I intend to see it through to the bitter end.

Growing up poor in America, it's almost inevitable that one has a very limited view of the world, especially if you are an African American. Every

February, as you know, is Black History Month, wherein we learn about, among other things, the Civil Rights movement and its leaders; but never is it expanded to include the Civil Rights movements in other countries. Therefore, I found it very interesting that Bobby's people were involved in a similar struggle as my own. And the fact that the Protestants and Catholics are pitted against each other seems eerily similar to how poor whites and blacks are pitted against each other here in America. And so a pattern begins to emerge: poor people being divided in order that they might be conquered by the rich! And the whole thing about Bobby not wanting to be identified as a "criminal," I responded very much to that. To the casual observer, of course, it would appear that he had taken it too far; after all, we're only talking about a pair of pants here, to which Bobby would no doubt reply: "Very good: you have grasped the situation. But not altogether. Because if it was only about a pair of pants, it wouldn't matter to them whether I wore them or not. No, this is about me (us) legitimizing their authority and practices and, at the same time, admitting that we are wrong in wanting to determine for ourselves what our lives should be." So I understand where he was coming from and where he was going, and I think he got there with everything intact. I cried that he had to die like that, but they weren't sad tears; they were mad tears (if you know what I mean).

Mr. O'Hearn, I feel really blessed to have read your book, to have learned about Bobby Sands and his comrades. As I said, I have met similar souls along the way. I have been fortunate enough to have been around men who, like Bobby, knew that life could be had no matter where you are. And with these men I have laughed, cried, struggled, strived, and, yes, we have sung together (smile). And you're right: it's nothing but an unfinished song... It's not over!

Sincerely,
Bomani Shakur

I was not sure if Mr. O'Hearn would respond to my letter, but a few weeks later I received a long reply to what I had written. We struck up a correspondence. In the months that followed, we talked about everything under the sun, from Karl Marx to John Coltrane, but mainly (and most importantly) we talked about what it meant to be alive.

He was a professor of sociology, I found out, and taught at university in Ireland and half a year in the States, in New York, at Binghamton University.

"You should come and see me sometime," I wrote to him, half-jokingly.

"I would love to," he replied. "Let me know what I have to do to get on your list."

I sent out some visiting forms, and he came to see me when next he was stateside.

I find it hard now to recapture the poignancy of that first face-to-face encounter. We met in the visiting room and sat on opposite sides of a glass partition, a barbaric barrier between two worlds. I smiled at him, amazed that I was sitting across from the author of *Nothing But An Unfinished Song*. But there he was, the acclaimed biographer and professor, smiling right back at me. We talked for six hours nonstop, pausing only to repeat ourselves over the clamor of disembodied voices that reverberated out of the adjoining booths. We spent Saturday and Sunday together, 12 hours total, and it was the first time in years that I did not have to talk about my case and why I had been sentenced to death. As it turned out, there were more important things to discuss....

"Have you ever read *The Sociological Imagination* by C. Wright Mills?" he wanted to know.

"Never heard of it."

"Well, I'll have to send it to you."

As the years went by, Mr. O'Hearn (or "Denis," as I came to know him) would send me tons and tons of literature to help enhance my scope and understanding of the human experience. With his tutelage, I was able to gain a better grasp of some of the social forces that contributed to the person I had become.

Never once during our lengthy conversations did we speak about my going on hunger strike or engaging in some other form of protest to win the right to touch my family. Our friendship forbade such suggestions. Still, I would be lying if I said the thought had not crossed my mind.

On a subsequent visit, he told me that he was on his way back to Ireland for a "short visit."

"Could you wear my necklace and place it on Bobby's grave?" I asked.

"Yes, of course, I can do that for you," he said, happy to oblige.

I looked at him and smiled. Did he know what I was up to? If so, he did not let on.

"I got something to tell you when you get back," I told him.

"Oh, yeah, what's that?" he asked, smiling.

"When you get back...."

On July 30, 2010, three years after the evidentiary hearing, Judge Merz issued his report and recommendation to District

Court Judge Thomas Rose. In complete contradiction to the image he had presented as an empathetic, objective mediator of the merits, he put forward a scathing, one-sided report that totally mischaracterized the facts.

With respect to the March 6, 1995, pre-trial hearing, wherein Judge Fred Crow refused to order the State to turn over the complete statements of inmates who claimed to have witnessed the murders inside of L-Block, Merz cited Judge Crow's halfhearted offer of more time and funding for additional investigators as proof of the State's satisfying its obligation under *Brady v. Maryland*. He failed to cite the State's refusal to match the actual names of witnesses with the statements that had been given, which was in total contradistinction to the law governing exculpatory evidence. Furthermore, he found that the statements that were *not* turned over "contained little that would have been non-cumulative and favorable to LaMar's defense."

To support this assertion, he cited the suppressed statement of Michael Jones, the inmate who claimed to have witnessed Frederick Frakes kill William Svette, and concluded that what Jones had to say was "merely cumulative," because an inmate named Robert Bass had already testified that Frakes murdered Svette in the L-corridor "after he was severely beaten in or near his cell and thought dead."

Again, this was a blatant mischaracterization of the facts. According to Jones, he was sitting in the corridor and saw Svette sit up and shake his head "like he was trying to clear cob-webs" and "got up on his own." He also stated that Svette "looked normal to me.... He didn't look like he was dying." This was not cumulative, and the jury should have been allowed to weigh the credibility of the State's witnesses next to the testimony of witnesses who offered competing versions of the facts.

Lastly, there was the withheld statement of James Edinbaugh, who claimed to have witnessed the deaths (in L-6) of Vitale, Depina, Staiano, and Svette. In his interview, he offered unequivocal exculpatory remarks that Judge Merz inexplicably ignored. With respect to whom the actual leader of the death squad was, Edinbaugh stated the following:

Question: Did the inmates mention why they were assaulting these particular inmates?

Answer: No, they didn't.

Q: Never said?

A: The only thing I got from that (inaudible) was that they was following Blackmon. Blackmon was the leader of the pack.

Q: Blackmon was the leader of the seven or eight that was in there [L-6]?

A: Right.

Q: How do you know he was the leader?

A: Because the way they was following him, the way he was gesturing and giving orders, you know.

Q: Okay, so Blackmon was giving the orders?

A: Right.

Hence, according to Edinbaugh, who never once mentioned my name, it was someone else who had played the very role that was assigned to me by the prosecution. And yet, Judge Merz concluded "nothing in Edinbaugh's statement undermines confidence in the verdicts returned in LaMar's case."

I was blown away by his merciless mischaracterization, especially since he had gone out of his way to be so affable and conciliatory at the hearing. A friend and supporter, Sharon Danann, wrote to me when she found out about Merz' recommendation:

21 November 2010
Dear Bomani:

The news about your appeal is somewhat shocking. I continue to be so naïve that it catches me off guard when someone like a judge is completely two-faced. Judge Merz was so friendly and welcoming to those of us who came to your hearing. But clearly he comes down on the wrong side of discovery, exculpatory evidence and the right of defendants to prove their innocence. Every time I hear, "Innocent until proven guilty," I go into a tirade....

This was the collective sentiment shared by all who had attended the hearing. How could he? The prosecution had shown such blatant disregard for the law that it seemed obvious to us that Merz had no choice but to rule in my favor, or, at the very least, grant me the opportunity to comb the prosecutors' files to further develop my claim. But the final word on the matter had not been said. My attorney, David Doughten, would be given the opportunity to file objections to these mischaracterizations and, if we were lucky, the district judge, as he had done with regard to statutory tolling, could reverse Judge Merz' decision.

On November 28, 2010, Mr. Doughten filed the final objections to Judge Merz' report and recommendations. When I read them, I was incensed by the haphazard way in which they were written. Not only did he fail to "object" to the magistrate's blatant mischaracterizations, but he rambled his way through an incoherent depiction of events that bore virtually no resemblance to what actually took place.

When Prosecutor Piepmeier took the stand during the evidentiary hearing, it was Mr. Doughten who had pinned him down and forced him to admit to applying a narrow *Brady* standard; but now, three years later, he seemed to have totally lost his grasp. *The fix is in*, I told myself, unable to comprehend how he could so carelessly mishandle my most important issue.

"I think you're sabotaging my case, David," I told him when he and Kate came to visit me.

"What?" he said, taken aback by the accusation. "What are you saying, Keith?" he asked, flustered.

"I'm saying you intentionally sabotaged my case—that's what I'm saying. How else do you explain the haphazard objections you filed? You were all over the place, and never once did you object to the judge's mischaracterizations! I want you off my case, David. You've taken my strongest issue and just squandered it," I said, unable to contain my frustration.

"But, Keith, even if we would have won, we'd still be exactly where we are right now; the State would have appealed and we would be in the Sixth Circuit."

"So you're sayin' it doesn't matter—is that what you're saying? 'Cause it matters to me whether or not you're fighting for my life. I want you off my case, man," I repeated.

"Well, if that's what you want, Keith, I'll have to respect

your decision; but I'm telling you, I really want to win your case...."

I was not convinced. I sat there and looked at him, and then at Kate, wondering how things had come to this. I held my head in my hands, fighting off a migraine, wanting to disappear.

"I just gotta get outta here, man," I said, ending the visit without reaching a resolution. "We'll talk about it some other time when I can think straight."

When Denis made it back to see me, he brought Bilge, his soon-to-be wife, along as an early Christmas present. I was happy to see them. They had already heard the news about the judge's decision and were visibly upset. When I told them about my suspicions regarding my attorney intentionally sabotaging my case, they grew quiet, registering the anger and frustration in my voice. Without really knowing what to think or say, they tried to console me.

"I'm going on a strike," I announced, matter-of-factly.

They looked at me with concern on their faces.

"About your legal situation?" Denis asked.

"No, no—I have to deal with that on my own, later," I said, rushing along. "I'm going on a hunger strike to force the administration to give me the same privileges as other death-row inmates," I explained. "I'm tired of sitting around here waiting on these people to have mercy on me. Shit, I'll be dead by the time they decide I deserve to touch my family again...."

"Yeah, well, if there's anything I can do," Denis said, "I'm with you, Bomani."

"I'm with you, too, Bomani," Bilge chimed in.

"I'm glad to hear that," I said, relieved to have their support. "I talked to Jason about it, and he doesn't think it's a good idea, said these people aren't going to give us anything. Alice said the same thing."

"What about the rest of the guys?" Denis asked.

"Well, Namir is a diabetic and won't be able to participate," I told him. "Hasan's on-board, though, and thinks we should rally the troops. I agree with him. If we're gonna pull this thing off, we're gonna need as much outside support as possible. I'ma need you to write something, too."

"Whatever you need, Bomani."

"I'ma also need my necklace back," I told him, smiling.

Denis O'Hearn wearing my necklace at the grave of Bobby Sands

"Yeah, I have it." And then, suddenly, he understood. "Oh, I see," he said, smiling back at me.

"Yeah, I'ma need Bobby with me on this one," I said, turning serious. "We might have to go all the way this time."

"You think so, huh?"

"I don't really know, man," I told him, honestly. "But this is my last year of sitting around like this. My little niece, Kayla, is eight years old now and pretty soon she'll be too big for me to pick up. I can't let that happen, man," I concluded, tears welling up in my eyes.

"Yeah, I hear you. I understand. Just let me know what you need me to do," Denis said.

In the ensuing weeks, Hasan and I "rallied the troops." We put a call out to our family, friends and supporters and told them about what we intended to do and, surprisingly, most of them were on board. The only sticking point was the date. We were shooting for December 1, 2010, which many believed was too short a notice with the Christmas holiday fast approaching.

"We need more time to coordinate our efforts," Sharon said. After much debate, we decided to put it off until January 2011. It turned out to be the right decision. The few extra weeks would give me the time to write a statement, a few words to put into perspective the agony of our situation and the unjust nature of the circumstances we were being subjected to. I felt that people needed to understand that we were being singled out and treated differently from other death-row inmates. To that end, I composed the following declaration:

If We Must Die

Before I speak my piece, let me make one thing perfectly clear: I don't want to die. I want to live and breathe and strive to do something righteous with my life. For the past 16 years I've been in solitary confinement, confined to a cell 23 hours a day for something I didn't do, and I have gone as far as I am willing to go.

Am I giving up? No. This is a protest, the only nonviolent way I can think of to express the deep disdain I have for the unjust situation that I am in. Make no mistake: my physical and mental strength are intact. However, to continue on in this way would be to lend legitimacy to a process that is both fraudulent and vindictive; this I am no longer willing to do.

I realize that for some of you the thought that an innocent man could be sent to prison and ultimately executed is inconceivable. But it happens. In a system that's based more on competition than on the equitable treatment of others, the football field is not the only place where participants are encouraged to win at any cost. Hence, in order to be victorious, some prosecutors hide evidence, lie in open court, and even pay for the perjured testimony of their witnesses. And this is exactly what happened in my case, and in the majority of cases stemming from the Lucasville Prison Uprising (1993).

But let us for the moment put aside the question of my guilt or innocence, because that, believe it or not, is not what this is about. On that score, we have written several books, produced a play and are putting the final touches on a full-scale documentary[15] to illustrate the travesty of justice

---

[15] "The Great Incarcerator, part 2: The Shadow of Lucasville," directed by D Jones, was released in April, 2013.

that has taken place here; and these things are available to you if you are interested. For now, I want to talk about dying....

In all that is presently unclear, one thing is certain: I have been sentenced to death, which, as you know, is the severest penalty known to man. Typically, when one has been given the death penalty, one is placed alongside other similarly-sentenced prisoners and they, together, are housed in an area that has been designated as Death Row. As living situations go, this is a very bleak and miserable place: men are sent here to die, to be killed by the State. No one in their right mind would ask to be sent here; and yet, this is precisely what I am asking, which should give you an indication of just how insufferable the situation I am living under is....

A few months ago, a federal judge recommended that my case be dismissed, which effectively moved me one step closer to being executed. It's hard to explain how this made me feel. However, if justice as a concept is real, then I could with some justification say, "Justice delayed is justice denied." But this has never been about justice, and I finally, finally, finally understand that. For the past 16 years, we have been nothing more than scapegoats for the State, a convenient excuse that they can point to whenever they need to raise the specter of fear among the public or justify the expenditure of inordinate amounts of money for more locks and chains.

And not only that, but the main reason behind the double penalty that we have been undergoing is so that we can serve as an example of what happens to those who challenge the power and authority of the State. And like good little pawns, we're supposed to sit here and wait until they take us to their death chamber, strap us down to a gurney, and pump poison through our veins....

At the beginning of this I wanted to make it perfectly clear that I did not want to die, and I don't. Life is a beautiful thing, especially when we are conscious of the value of it. However, if we must die, we should be allowed to do so with dignity, which is all we're asking: the opportunity to pursue our appeals unimpeded, to be able to touch our friends and families, and to no longer be treated as playthings but as human beings who are facing the ultimate penalty.

Therefore, in the words of Claude McKay, I share the following as my parting sentiments:

If we must die, let it not be like hogs
Hunted and penned in an inglorious spot,
While round us bark the mad and hungry dogs,
Making their mock at our accursed lot.
If we must die, O let us nobly die,
So that our precious blood may not be shed
In vain; then even the monsters we defy
Shall be constrained to honor us though dead!
O kinsmen! We must meet the common foe!
Though far outnumbered let us show us brave,
And for their thousand blows deal one death-blow!
What though before us lies the open grave?
Like men we'll face the murderous, cowardly pack,
Pressed to the wall, dying, but fighting back!

* * * * *

Though initially reluctant, Jason joined Hasan and me in the trenches when the hunger strike began on January 3, 2011. The following are excerpts from the journal I kept to chronicle the daily developments surrounding our plight:

January 3: just refused my first tray; the hunger strike has officially begun! It'll take three days before these people consider it a legitimate strike. I wonder how long it'll take for them to realize that we are serious? Already there's been a news broadcast announcing our demonstration, which is somewhat surprising given that we've only begun.

The warden, on his rounds a few days ago, stopped and asked Hasan if we were going on a strike, and Hasan asked him why he thought that, and the warden responded, "Because it's all over the Internet." This is going to be interesting.

January 5: just came back from a visit with my friends, Denis and Bilge. Feeling extremely encouraged. They told me that support is building around the world. Hard to imagine that, but it's a hopeful indication that we'll be able to garner some much-needed attention. This whole thing will probably come down to whether or not people get involved. We just have to hope that that is the case. Sharon is also working hard to spread the word, as well as Alice and Staughton. So we'll see. For now, I'm trying to stay focused and keep my mind off food!

January 6: just came back from the nurse. It's official: we're now on hunger strike. The nurse told me that my blood pressure was unusually high—140 over 90—and then went on to tell me the effects of not eating. Seemed like he was trying to scare me. If so, it didn't work. I imagine the warden will be down to see us today or tomorrow. Supposedly, a team will be put together to talk to us about our demands, etc. We've already decided not to speak to anyone except the warden. He's the one with the power to meet our demands, so he's the one we'll talk to, period. Feeling pretty good so far. There was another announcement on the news.

Just spoke to Warden Bobby and Deputy Warden Remmick. The warden was holding the letter I wrote to him stating our demands. He said he would seriously consider our concerns, but added that "as long as you're on strike, it's unlikely that anything will change." When I reminded him that we'd been down here for almost 13 years and nothing has changed, he tried to tell me how good we've had it compared to our tenure under other wardens. He then tried to narrow me down to one or two demands by asking, "Which one or two are the most important?" I told him, "They're all equally important." Remmick chimed in and said, "Now that you are a bigshot," referring to the news coverage. I ignored him. The warden said I should trust him, to which I replied, "Trust is earned."

January 7: received a copy of the article Denis wrote in the [Youngstown] *Vindicator*.[16] Powerful piece!

---

[16] http://www.vindy.com/news/2011/jan/03/on-hunger-strike-to-be-on-death-row/

Said I was closer to him than "any man on earth." Wow—that's really something to say. I feel the same way about him. Been receiving mail from all over the world, people telling me that they support what we are doing. Wow! Sharon wrote and told me that people are bombarding her with requests to speak on the radio, write articles, and so on.

January 8: just came back from visiting with Uncle Mannie; good visit....

January 9: slow day today. No mail, no movement— nothing! Spent the whole day looking out the window and reading some of Nazim Hikmet's poetry:

> I live in a world of forbidden things!
> To smell your lover's cheek: forbidden!
> To talk with your brother or mother
> without a wire screen or guard
> between you: forbidden.
> And not that it isn't forbidden,
> but what you can hide in your heart
> and have in your hand,
> is to love, think, and understand.

*****

January 10: refused to see the nurse today. Not in the mood for his scare-tactics. Received tons of mail and messages from all over the country and the world—Serbia, Ireland, Amsterdam, England. What is this? Surely this is forbidden! These people have done an excellent job in making us believe that we are alone and beyond help; but how quickly that is being made into a lie. And it's the same for everybody, everywhere: this system thrives on making us feel separated and alone. Divided, they rule us. People have to take the chance to reach out. Who knows, maybe an echo will penetrate the darkness.

January 11: spoke to Alice and Staughton today; they say things are going better than expected. Still, I could hear the concern in their voices, although they were both kind enough not to try to discourage me. Love them very much. Feeling tired, been sleeping all day today. They turned me down at the privilege review—surprise, surprise. Warden Bobby and Remmick just came around with the lunch trays (a coincidence?), telling us no matter how long we're on the strike, they're not going to deal with us. We'll see. I'm down to 197 lbs. Lost 13 pounds so far.

January 12: no mail—nothing! Got word from Hasan that they aired another news broadcast, but "Your name wasn't mentioned. These people really seem to have a hard on for you...." I wonder what that means—are they saying I'm no longer on the strike? Crazy! Got word that Remmick threatened to take away the current privileges that we have in order to force us off the strike. Hearing the news, I posted the following communiqué:

RE: 5A Long-term Privileges
Mr. Remmick:

It comes as no surprise that you have resorted to even more vindictiveness as a way to break our resolve. You would think that after 12 years that you would know us better than that; but then again, the recent move to take away the miniscule privileges that we have left says more about you than it does about us. Therefore, to lessen the possibility of further confusion, I'd like to make arrangements to have the rest of my "privileges" sent home. I've already sent home my television set and will gladly have my family pick up the rest of my personal belongings. I have an assortment of books, a CD-player, and other sundry items in storage—please, at your soonest convenience, could you have Sgt. Johns round these things up and make them available for any one of the several visitors I have this weekend?

January 13: just received a letter from Alice telling me that she suspects that they will meet "some, if not all, of our demands." And what do you know, not even an hour later we were called out to speak with Warden Bobby and Remmick, and just as Alice had predicted they agreed to everything with only a few, very small concessions. Unbelievable! As Warden Bobby was going down the list, I showed a little impatience and reminded him that he had not said anything about semi-contact visits yet, which elicited a smile from him. "I know, I know," he said, chuckling. "Yes, we're going to give you semi-contact visits." I looked at Remmick when he said this, and I could tell by the reddening of his neck that he was upset (smile). He immediately chimed in, "But we're gonna piss test you on a regular basis." Unfortunately, one of the demands that Warden Bobby would not consider was Remmick's resignation, which was belatedly added by Hasan.

When Warden Bobby refused to discuss the matter, Hasan requested to be taken back to his cell. Jason seemed pleased with how things had turned out, as was I. There was just one minor detail to discuss. "We're gonna need everything in writing," I said. To this, the warden threw his head back as if he had been slapped in the face. "Oh, you don't trust me?" And then Jason chimed in, enumerating the various instances when promises had been made and forgotten after a period of time. Surprisingly, without further discussion, the warden promised to provide us with the list of agreed-upon privileges in writing. "I'm not coming off until I see it," I said.

January 14: had a wonderful visit with Alice and Staughton. Told them about the warden's proposal, and they both seemed genuinely surprised, although I suspect that they had something to do with it. How else would they have known that an offer was coming? They both knew how important semi-contact visits were to me, and the news brought big smiles to their faces. And then the bad news: "We received word from Kate that the district judge turned down your appeal. She asked us to tell you." I wasn't expecting that one. "So what now?" I asked Staughton. "Well, we roll up our sleeves and fight," he said. Exactly what I was thinking. We finished the visit off by singing *We Shall Overcome*. When I made it back to the cell, I found the memo from Warden Bobby lying on the bed. As promised, he put everything in writing. I guess that's it, then. I'll wait to hear from Hasan before I do anything. I'll see him tomorrow. Received word that Jason just accepted his lunch tray (smile)! Pretty good day today, all things considered. Even with the bad news, there's still so much to be proud about. We set out to accomplish something and stuck together. That's what's up! But, of course, we could not have done it without all the love and support from the outside. I guess Richard Wright was right after all: "If you possess the courage to speak out what you are, you will find that you are not alone!" Amen to that.

January 15: Victory day! Didn't sleep a wink last night; too excited. The visit with our supporters went well after a few minor disagreements. Hasan thought we should continue on the strike even though the demands had been met; in the end, however, we all agreed that it was time to shift perspectives and start focusing on the larger task of overturning our wrongful convictions. Just spoke with Alice and Staughton, and they informed me that the rally was a BIG success. They said people were energized and fired up about the fact that we finally achieved a small victory. Just ate four hot dogs! Probably shouldn't have done that, but I couldn't help myself. Never tasted so good! It's been a helluva ride, and the only words I can summon to capture the poignancy of the moment come from a poem by Nazim Hikmet:

This Journey

We open doors,
close doors,
pass through doors,
and reach at the end of our only journey
no city,
no harbor—
the train derails
the ship sinks
the plane crashes.
The map is drawn on ice.
But if I could
begin this journey all over again,
I would.

*****

The jubilation I felt at having achieved such a stupendous victory left me dizzy. It was hard to believe that in just 12 days we were able to accomplish what, for 16 years, we had been told would NEVER happen. How easily we had accepted that lie! When the administration refused to follow their own rules, we complained (verbally and informally), and then asked a district judge to intervene on our behalf, all to no avail. It never occurred to us that we were wasting our time by appealing to the very people who had placed us in the predicament we were in.

Indeed, the whole process of redressing our grievances was nothing more than an exercise in futility designed to drain off our vital energy and make us feel as though we had done all that we could do.

It was only when we began to write and reach out to "the people" that things began to change. First, there was Staughton's book and an accompanying play; then we began holding "talks" around the state on various college campuses, as well as writing articles in various periodicals. In this way, we were able to generate some much-needed support. Still, even with all the progress we had made, none of us expected the overwhelming outpouring that occurred.

When the hunger strike was over, I wanted to write to each and every person who had reached out to me. However, by the time all was said and done, I had received well over 100 letters and emails (not to mention the 1,000 or so signatures on a petition that called for the immediate end to the "cruel and unusual punishment" we were being subjected to). Since it seemed impossible to write to each and every person, I composed an open "love letter" to all those who had supported us, making sure they understood that it was only through their love and support that things had changed:

Power to the People

Although on a very small scale (which by no means diminishes the deed), we, the people, have wrought a revolution—"a sudden and momentous change in a situation"—and accomplished in 12 days what the powers that be have repeatedly told us would never happen. Indeed, for the first time in 16 years, I will be able to hug and kiss my family again! There are no words to express the profound gratitude I feel.

The late, great, revolutionary leader, Che Guevara, once said: "A true revolutionary is guided by great feelings of love!" Well, while I cannot claim to be a revolutionary in the strict sense of the word, it is a great feeling of love—for you, the people—that is guiding me right now: even as I write this, tears of hope and determination are streaming down my face.

When one has been forced to live in a space no larger than a closet for 16 years, 23 hours a day, not only does one begin to feel extremely insignificant, but the very world begins to shrink; and everything, even the smallest thing, seems impossible. Hence, never in my wildest dreams could I have imagined the overwhelming outpouring of love and support that came flooding into my cell after I cried out for help. People from all over the country and the world—England, Ireland, Serbia, The Netherlands—reached out and joined together with us to right an injustice; and surprisingly, miraculously, we succeeded! Everything we demanded was promptly handed over.

It would be great if I could say that the worst is over now, and that, with victory in hand, I can live happily ever after. Unfortunately, I don't have the luxury of living in a fairy tale; the people who are trying to take my life are real, not a figment of my imagination. In fact, not even a week after my piece—"If We Must Die"—was posted and we embarked on the hunger strike, a federal district judge turned down my appeal, which placed me even further in the balance. It would be naïve of me to believe that this was just a coincidence, an unrelated incident that just so happened to coincide with our peaceful, nonviolent demonstration. As you may recall, I said some very harsh things (all of them true) against the system; and I say them again: this system is bogus and sold to those with money. In other words, if you don't have the capital you get the punishment, and justice, like everything else in this capitalistic nightmare, is nothing more than a commodity that is reserved for the highest bidder....

Friends, we don't have to accept this; we don't have to continue down the path of least resistance, allowing them to do with us whatever they please. If we stand together and speak truth to power, they will have no choice but to right this wrong. They did it in the current confrontation, and they will do it again, not because they want to but because they have to. Whenever hypocrisy is confronted by the truth, it must capitulate. Therefore, the key to fighting these people is to expose the truth and then hold it up next to what they claim to represent. If we can do this well enough, they will either have to practice what they preach or, as Malcolm X suggests, preach what they practice. Our job is to make sure that they don't have it both ways.

In closing, I want to thank each and every one of you for coming forward as you did. I am both humbled and uplifted by the support. When I phoned my eight-year-old niece, Kayla, and informed her that "Uncle Keith will be able to touch your little hand soon," she—with excitement brimming in her voice—said, "That's awesome!" And I couldn't agree with her more: what we did was awesome! We came together and spoke truth to power and won! Imagine that!

Power to the People!

Bomani Shakur a.k.a. Keith LaMar
January 2011

A year after being granted semi-contact visits,
we were granted full-contact visits, and I **FINALLY**
got to pick up my then ten-year-old niece, Kayla.

Turning back to my legal troubles was a definite downer after experiencing the thrill of such unbridled interest and enthusiasm, but I had to do it. I could not bury my head in the sand and pretend that everything was all right.

I met with Kate on a cold February morning and we had a very long discussion about where things currently stood now that the district judge had turned down my appeal. I would be going into the Sixth Circuit Court of Appeals, she explained, which was basically my last hope for relief. If I did not receive a favorable ruling there, it was all but certain that

I would be executed. I nodded my head as she explained things, wondering all along when were we going to address the elephant in the room.

"So what about this thing with David?" I finally asked, unable to contain my impatience.

"What d'you mean?" she asked, as if she did not already know.

"About him sabotaging my case, Kate," I said, frowning.

"Keith, I don't believe David is trying to sabotage your case," she said, with a somber expression.

"Well, how do you explain the objections he filed, Kate?" I asked.

"I don't know what to tell you, Keith," she said, looking flustered. "David is—"

"Did you even read 'em, Kate?" I asked, wondering how she could sit there and defend the indefensible.

"Well, no, I haven't read them. I—"

"You haven't read them?" I asked, cutting her off. "You mean I've been going on and on about this and you haven't even taken the time to read them?" I asked again, fixing her with an incredulous stare.

"Well, I have other cases, Keith," she informed me. "You're not my only client."

"So I'm not a priority, in other words. Is that what you're saying?"

"Keith."

It was a low blow, said more out of frustration than out of actual belief. I never once doubted that Kate had my best interest in mind. Even with my suspicions about David, I was still convinced that I could nevertheless count on her. And now I had hurt her feelings.

"I'm sorry, Kate," I said, offering her a contrite apology.

She was silent.

"Listen, I understand that you have other clients, but this

is very important to me, Kate," I told her, regaining my composure. "I need to go into this last phase knowing that I can trust my attorneys, and I don't trust him, Kate."

Silence.

"He didn't even object to the judge's mischaracterizations," I went on, pleading my case. "He let stand as fact things that weren't even true.... Please, when you get back, can you at least look at what he did and tell me if it was up to par? That's all I'm asking."

"I'll take a look at it, Keith," she said, coming back around. "I meant to do that after our last visit, but I didn't. I'll take a look at it and get back to you, okay?"

"Yeah, okay. Let me know what you think," I said, feeling somewhat relieved.

A few days later, I received a letter from David:

March 5, 2011
Dear Mr. LaMar:

I spoke with Katie yesterday. I am sorry that you still think that I sabotaged your issue. I had thought that we had worked this out when I was down there. I am glad that you are at least comfortable that Katie did not. I do not know what to tell you. I want very badly to win your case, as I do everyone's case whom I represent. But because of the violations in discovery in your matter I may want to win even more to expose the tricks....

Again, I was not convinced. His whole manner of reassuring me gave me the sense that I was being accosted by a used car salesman who was trying to sell me a lemon.

A month after our visit, Kate wrote to me:

April 1, 2011
Dear Keith:

I did what you asked. I reviewed the objections to the R&R [report and recommendation]. It seemed like an appropriate time, since I was looking at various documents to prepare the application for a COA [certificate of appealability]. I agree that we could have done a better job. Objections are odd pleadings, because you need to tell the district court why the magistrate was wrong. In your case, the magistrate was wrong on the facts and law. I guess I would again ask that you consider all the work that both Dave and I have done on your case and excuse this one document that could have been better. I sensed from our conversation you felt that it made a difference in the outcome of your case. I disagree....

I was glad that Kate had kept her word and read the objections; still, the fact was not lost on me that she had written her letter on April Fool's Day. I wrote her a curt reply:

5 April 2011
Dear Kate:

I haven't had the chance to read the COA yet. I wanted to write you this quick letter to let you know that it meant a lot to have your words of assurance. For the record, I never actually lost faith in you and in your ability to represent me. Like you, I was unnerved by and after our last encounter. To arrive at this critical juncture in the process and not be able to completely trust in the work that is being done on my behalf is deeply disturbing; and while it upset me that we had to fuss and fight, I was even more upset that it had to come to that.

Listen, Kate, I don't know how much work David has actually done on my case. My understanding is that most of the work has already been done and we're basically sticking to our guns (so to speak) by preserving and refining the key issues as we go forward. In your letter you ask that I "excuse" the haphazard way in which David approached the *Brady* issue, and, to be perfectly candid, I find that to be an unreasonable request. I can excuse the misspelled words and shabby syntax; however, the fact that he dealt so carelessly with what is perhaps my most winnable issue is inexcusable!

Look, I'm not an attorney, so I won't insult your intelligence by explaining your job to you. However, I'd ask that you not insult my intelligence by asking me to believe that David's failure to object to the judge's obvious mischaracterizations of the facts was harmless. I believe you would feel differently if it were your life that was on the line. With that said, I see no sense in belaboring the point, so long as you understand where I stand....

I wanted David off my case. However, after our disputatious exchange, it was mutually decided that he would defer to Kate and allow her to take the lead on the *Brady* issue. Since there was no way for me to prove he had intentionally sabotaged my case, I let the matter drop for the time being. It was an uneasy truce, one that I would come to regret when, several months later, I came to Kate and asked her to file what I felt was an important motion to redress the erroneous ruling that Judge Merz had made.

As it turned out, Merz was also the magistrate judge on Hasan's case and, as he had done for me, had "recommended" that Hasan's petition be similarly dismissed. However, unlike District Judge Rose who presided over my case and seemed to rubberstamp virtually everything Judge Merz sent to him, Hasan had a different district judge—Chief Judge Susan J. Dlott—who would ultimately take a different stance on what was revealed during my evidentiary hearing.

On November 17, 2011, District Judge Dlott granted Hasan leave to obtain limited discovery, based almost entirely on the fact that Mr. Piepmeier, while being deposed by my attorneys, admitted to applying what District Judge Dlott termed a "narrow *Brady* standard" to determine what evidence to turn over to the defense. Based on this, Hasan was granted leave to obtain the following discovery:

- Records depositions of the Ohio State Highway Patrol (OSHP);
- To obtain the computer-generated index of witness statements, created and maintained by OSHP;
- The [OSHP] database burned to a CD by the OSHP;
- Access to the original version of the database be provided by the OSHP;
- Upon request, access to the interview summaries and transcripts still maintained by the OSHP at the facilities on Alum Creek Dr., Columbus, Ohio;
- Copies of video depositions and transcripts of same in the possession of OSHP;
- Transcripts and/or tape recordings of RIB hearings in the possession of DRC;
- Copies of the video depositions of each of the witnesses that testified at petitioner's trial....
- Copies of the audiotapes of each of the witnesses

that testified at petitioner's trial, including: Stacey Gordon, Interview No. 1326 Tate No. 194;

- Copies of any audio or videotapes prepared by the special prosecutor or the OSHP during the Lucasville Investigation relevant to the murder of C.O. Vallandingham.

This was a tremendous coup for Hasan and his attorneys. In effect, Judge Dlott reversed Judge Merz' recommendation and allowed Hasan access to the Holy Grail.

"You've gotta get with your attorneys and make sure they get on board with this," Hasan told me.

"Yeah, I hear you," I said, not wanting to get drawn into a long discussion about it. "I'll take care of it."

I was happy for him, of course. I was also a little bewildered by the fact that it had been as a result of something that had been revealed at my hearing that Hasan was now being granted leave to obtain this much-coveted material. *If anybody should benefit from what Mr. Piepmeier said, it should be me,* I thought, somewhat selfishly. However, thinking about the big altercation I just had with my attorneys made me reluctant to risk another fight with them so soon. It was a ridiculous thought: I should have felt free to approach my own attorneys with news that could have possibly benefitted my case. But I resolved to hold my tongue.

And then, on February 24, 2012, Judge Merz granted George Skatzes leave to obtain discovery, stating: "It seems inappropriate, in the absence of very persuasive argument to the contrary, for this Court to constrain discovery in this case arising out of the same factual circumstances if district judges of the Court have granted parallel requests."

Hearing the news, Hasan once again implored me to get

involved.

"I don't know what's your problem, Bomani," he said, looking at me as if I was retarded or something, "but this is what we've been waiting on...."

I nodded my head in agreement. By now, Namir, too, had been granted discovery after his attorneys intervened in Jason's case, who was the first to receive extended discovery. Now all four of them—Jason, Hasan, Namir, and George—were waiting on their attorneys to scour the vast database that had been compiled by the Ohio State Highway Patrol. As always, I was the odd man out, feeling indecisive, wondering what I should do.

Finally, after taking the time to read the orders in both Jason and Hasan's cases, I posted a letter to my attorneys:

26 August '12
Dear Kate and David:

In the past few weeks, since receiving notice of our briefing schedule, I have spoken with both Hasan and Jason Robb regarding the ongoing discovery that they have been allowed to pursue in their cases. In fact, it is my understanding that each of the four prisoners who have been sentenced to death as a result of the riot are now party to the extended discovery that was granted. Over the past week or so, I have read the orders in both of their cases (which have been consolidated) and have come to the conclusion that I, too, should be part of this collective effort to ascertain whether or not the State, in following its limited scope of what constituted exculpatory evidence, neglected to turn over something that could very well prove my innocence.

As you both are aware, the very crux of my case

turns on whether or not the State was remiss in refusing to turn over complete statements, and I feel that being party to this extended discovery can only bolster my claim. Therefore, I am hereby officially requesting that you both look into this matter with the view of filing the necessary motions that will, first of all, hold the briefing schedule in abeyance and, secondly, have my case remanded to the District Court for further consideration. I'm aware that the likelihood of a favorable ruling is probably slim to none; however, I want it on record that I, at the very least, tried to protect my rights....

A few weeks later, Kate responded:

September 17, 2012
Dear Keith:

I am writing in response to your letter of August 26, 2012, which I received last night.

I am aware of the discovery litigation in the other 4 cases. As you know, we did get a fair amount of discovery in your case, without being involved in the litigation and at that time we were constantly asking for additional discovery as it became known to us. In fact, I think that some of the discovery requests made in the other cases came as a result of the discovery we shared with the other attorneys in the cases, and we shared with the Lynds. I will go back over the discovery requests made in the other cases and we can discuss it when I see you. I am not opposed to filing a Motion to Remand; I just have not seen the basis to do so given my discussions with other Lucasville attorneys. As you know, your case is different than the other four, since your alleged crimes were completed at the beginning of the riot and the other cases revolved around the killing of the guard....

Again, I was glad that Kate had taken the time to respond to my letter (Mr. Doughten never even bothered). However, I did not agree with her assessment of things. Yes, my case was different than the other four, but the "narrow *Brady* standard" that had been devised by Mr. Piepmeier was applied across the board in each of our respective cases and, notwithstanding the death of the guard, deprived each of us of a fair trial. In fact, I had belatedly "discovered" a list of statements that had never been turned over to me by the State (See Appendix II); and being granted access to the OSHP database was the only way to determine whether or not any of these statements were exculpatory.

I could not understand why Kate and David were trying so hard to deter me from pursuing my rights; as my lawyers, they should have been on board with the rest of the attorneys who were fighting for their clients. Instead, they were fighting me every step of the way.

When Kate came to visit, I came out prepared to argue my case. It angered me that I had to try to convince her to do her job. *This is crazy,* I thought, as I sat down in the visiting booth opposite her.

"Hi Keith," she said, sticking out her hand.

"I came out here to convince you to file those motions, Kate," I told her, shaking her hand and getting right down to business.

"Yeah, I know," she said, looking pensive. "As I said, I really don't see the basis for it, but let me play devil's advocate."

"Alright," I said, a bit annoyed that she had started off by trying to dissuade me.

"What if we're granted the motion for leave and the judge doesn't allow us to use the material that we find?" she began.

"Why would he grant us leave and then prevent us from using the material?" I asked, confused.

"Well, what if the material isn't any good?"

"Then we're no worse off than we are now," I answered, irritated by her inane line of questioning.

"They're never going to grant this motion, Keith," she said, looking triumphant, as if she had proven her point.

"They granted it in all the other cases!" I exclaimed, raising my voice. "What makes you think they won't grant it for us?" I asked.

"Well, your case is different than theirs," she said.

"It's the same prosecutor, Kate, who created the criteria that determined what constituted exculpatory evidence; that's what this is all about, not whether or not I had something to do with the guard's death. What the hell, Kate!" I yelled, frustrated by her unwillingness to see the obvious.

"Why are you screaming at me?" she asked, startled by my outburst.

"I'm not screaming at you!" I yelled. "I'm screaming at the devil! Are you Kate now?" I asked.

"Yes, I'm Kate now," she said.

It was a weird exchange, and she seemed intent on making it weirder.

"They're going to get us on the Weaver thing," she said, referring to Dennis Weaver, the inmate who was killed while in the 10-man cell.

I looked at her. I was stunned.

"Why would you say something like that?" I asked. "I didn't kill Dennis."

She immediately seemed remorseful and tried to apologize for what she had said.

"Listen, Kate, while we're sitting here arguing, all the other attorneys are combing the database to see what the State didn't turn over. That's what we should be doing. And if they get us on the 'Weaver thing,' so be it. I just want to fight for my life—that's all."

"I'll file the motion, Keith," she said, with a tone of reconciliation.

"You mean that?" I asked, looking hopeful.

"Yes."

"I have your word?" I asked.

"Yes, you have my word," she promised.

I held out my hand and she took it.

"I just want to fight for my life, Kate," I repeated.

"I know, Keith."

When I made it back to the pod, I called Alice and Staughton and informed them of the news.

"Oh, that's great, Keith!" they exclaimed in unison.

"Yeah," I agreed, cautiously optimistic.

I was still a bit apprehensive, not knowing if Kate would keep her word. Things had become rather contemptuous between us and I did not know how she felt. In an attempt to reassure her that there were no hard feelings, I sat down and wrote her a letter:

4 October, '12
Dear Kate:

If after all is said and done and I am not successful, I won't blame you. I won't say, "It's your fault." My goal is to do everything reasonably possible to preserve my life. I'm well aware that our best efforts may come to naught; but then again, I can die tonight in my sleep. Such is life: we have no way of knowing when or how our lives will end. However, the unpredictability of life aside, there's such a thing as peace of mind, the state that comes from knowing that every remedy was exhausted—and that's all I ask, no more or less than what you yourself would expect if you were in my shoes. I'm glad you aren't in my shoes, by the way. I wouldn't wish this on my worst enemy.

You may think I don't appreciate all the work you have done on my behalf, but I'm aware that, given the circumstances, you are doing your best; that's all I ask, and that you continue to do so. When we come to the end of the road, I want us to be able to look into each other's eyes and know that everything was done. You understand?

I have nothing personal against you or David, and I hope neither you nor David have anything personal against me.... I'm not looking to shame or blame anyone; that's not my intentions at all. I want access to that database—something tells me that there's something there that will shine a new light on things. Will it matter? I have no idea. But, as I said, my goal is to exhaust my remedies, to do the most and best I can do. Whatever happens after that, I'm prepared to see things through to the bitter end if need be. Until then, I hope I can rely on your word to assist me in obtaining this extended discovery. I hope you won't abandon me at this most critical point. I hope we can remain on good terms (as opposed to becoming enemies). And, finally, I hope you know that I wish you nothing but the best, Kate.

Kate never responded to my letter. Instead, she arranged a conference call between her, David and me. I immediately knew something was wrong. *She's not going to keep her word*, I thought as I made my way to the conference room.

"Hello?" I said, speaking into the phone.

"Yes, Keith, this is Kate and David," Kate intoned, sounding professional.

"U-huh," I muttered, feeling anxious.

Without delay, she launched into a diatribe about how I was "being unduly influenced by the Lynds."

"What?" I gasped, surprised by her unfounded accusation. "What are you talking about? What do the Lynds have to do with anything?"

"Well, we're wondering who put you up to this," David said, interjecting himself into the conversation.

"No one put me up to anything, David," I said, instantly becoming angry. "What are you saying, that I'm too dumb to understand the importance of having access to the database; is that what you're saying?"

"Oh, no, no, I'm not saying you're dumb, Keith," he said. "I just want to know who put you up to this, that's all."

"I already told you nobody put me up to anything," I repeated, wondering where Kate had gone. She had grown noticeably silent.

"You sure the Lynds didn't put you up to this?" David asked.

I listened to him, growing angrier and angrier by the minute. Then, all of a sudden, I understood. *He's trying to get me to say something incriminating about the Lynds.* Without responding to his question, I hung up the phone.

I walked back to the cell in a daze. The guards who were escorting me noticed my somber mood and surmised that I had just received news that someone had died.

"Sorry for your loss," one of them chimed in, breaking through my reverie.

I looked at him with a puzzled expression, and then I understood.

"Oh, no, that was my attorneys," I said, shuffling down the hallway in handcuffs and shackles.

When I made it back to the cell, I sat down on the bed and leaned my head back against the wall. I took a deep breath. *What a bizarre experience*, I thought to myself. I had always felt that David did not give a damn about whether I lived or died, so it was not the exchange with him that had blown my mind. It was Kate who had caught me off guard. I thought I knew her; I thought she had my best interest at heart. A few days later, I received a letter from her addressed to "Mr. LaMar," something she had not called me in years. When I noticed the formality of it, my heart sank.

October 22, 2012
Dear Mr. LaMar:

I am enclosing a copy of the memo we have sent the Lynds regarding their participation in your case. I realize that you had hoped we could all work together on your behalf, but we do not see eye to eye with them on how to best represent you. The bottom line is that David and I are the ones appointed as your lawyers.

Having two sets of lawyers is not working. We feel that since the decision issued in the district court, that the Lynds have poisoned you against us. David and I have spent a great deal of time trying to explain federal habeas and legal concepts to the Lynds. It has taken away time from preparation of your appeal and it is now going to stop.

David and I want to win your case. We believe in the issues present in your case and believe that in spite of the fact that this is a "Lucasville case" that we can win and should win. To that end, we have consulted with experts around the country concerning how to proceed and are in the process of preparing your brief....

I was speechless. Just a week or so before receiving her letter, she and David had asked the Lynds to file a motion on my behalf in state court—and now, all of a sudden, they were the enemy? I did not understand it. I merely requested that she and David file a motion so that I could be party to the extended discovery that had been granted to the four other death-sentenced prisoners. If, indeed, she and David wanted to "win" my case, it seemed to me that a first step toward achieving that victory revolved around the strengthening of the *Brady* claim. What "experts around the country" would advise against being afforded the opportunity to review the voluminous list of withheld statements that could very well tip the scale in my favor?

"What's this all about, Kate?" I asked when I finally got ahold of her. "You gave me your word—"

"Hey! Hey! Hey!" she screamed, cutting me off. "We think the Lynds are unduly influencing you, and we're not going to have it any longer!"

"What are you talking about?" I asked, genuinely perplexed. "You just wrote the Lynds last week and asked them to file a motion on my behalf," I reminded her, baffled by her attitude.

"Oh, we were just bluffing," she told me, breathing heavily into the phone. "We knew they wouldn't file it."

I got quiet after she said that, thinking to myself how sad the whole thing was.

"Okay, Kate," I said, bringing an end to the call.

I could not believe things had come to this. Looking back over all that I had gone through, everything that I had endured and conquered, the last thing I expected was to be hindered by my own attorneys. I felt betrayed. *Maybe I should just turn over my appeals and let 'em kill me,* I said to myself, feeling defeated. But why do that? I had done nothing wrong. Indeed, for the first time in my life, I was right. I knew I was right, and I could not bring myself to think or feel otherwise. For weeks I walked around in a blue funk, feeling like a dead man, a ghost, wishing I could somehow disappear.

I knew that I would never be able to trust in Kate again, even though she and David would continue to represent me. They had done enough to meet the minimal standard of competency, so, unless they recused themselves, I was stuck with them. "If I had money," I told her during our last conversation, "I would fire you and David." She chuckled into the phone at that. Yes, they were free from having to suffer the consequences of their inactions. And this is how it always is: the poor must accept what they have to accept. It was a crushing realization, one that I had long come to terms with. Though it was my life on the line, I had no say in what should be done to preserve it. If they were wrong, oh well. I would die and they would go on with their careers as if nothing had happened. *How could they do that? How could they live with themselves?* I wondered.

Still, as much as I would like to, I cannot in good conscience lay all the blame on them. After all, Kate and David are not the ones who wrongfully indicted me; Mark Piepmeier did that. He was also the one who had created the "narrow *Brady* standard" that made it impossible for me to put on a defense. And then there were Seth Tieger and Bill Anderson, the two prosecutors who had gone out of their way not to be "the ones" to afford me a fair trial; yes, they were definitely derelict in their duty to uphold the Constitution. And let us not forget the Honorable Judge Crow, who colluded with the prosecution by allowing them to proffer statements without the corresponding names of the witnesses who had given them. In the almost 19 years since my trial, I still have not met one person who has ever heard of such a thing. And then there was Warden Tate, who set this whole thing in motion by refusing to offer Muslim inmates an alternative method by which they could be tested for TB.[17] Ultimately, a large portion of the blame must rest with him since he was the one who had the power to choose a different response.

And I, too, deserve some of the blame. When I refused to accept the "deal," I had no idea what the process of justice entailed. In all my years of dealing with the criminal justice system, I had never demanded a trial: I was always guilty of the crimes for which I had been charged. And somehow, because I had admitted my guilt, I concluded that the criminal justice system was just. Oh, how naïve I was! I actually convinced myself that there was no way a jury would find me guilty of these crimes. Indeed, when Michael Childers took the stand and claimed to have had microscopic microchips embedded in his brain, the jury laughed. And I laughed with them, never suspecting that the joke was on me. When they found me guilty and recommended that I be put to death, I was shocked. I really was. But I should not have been. I should have known better. I should have accepted the deal...

But had I done that, had I willingly forsaken myself, I

---

[17] As of this writing, ODRC, in an effort to save money, has discontinued mandatory TB testing of inmates, relying on a written survey of symptoms to detect whether or not inmates are infected.

would have never learned the truth about who I am. In fact, not accepting the deal was the pivot of my existence; it turned my life completely around. In time I came to understand what it means to have the courage of my convictions. I discovered that moral strength is far greater than physical strength and that, as Martin Luther King, Jr. suggested, "the ultimate measure of a man is not where he stands in moments of comfort and convenience, but where he stands at times of challenge and controversy." Through my challenges, I came to realize that I could count on myself, that I could trust in the goodness of others, and that I could rely on the efficacy of my own mind. Indeed, the truth about who I am is that I am a child of God, an extension of the universe; as such, I CANNOT BE DESTROYED. Yes, I can be beaten, starved, killed even; and yet, I am not my body, but the soul that dwells within. All of this I had to learn the hard way, through experience, but I learned it—and that is the most important thing.

Going forward, I would once again have to grope my way through darkness, in search of truth, understanding, and forgiveness. But I would not go quietly into that dark night as so many others had done. No, I would find a way to rise to the occasion. I would write my story. I would reach into the pain of my experience and share the shame that comes along with being poor, unequal, and despised. And I would tell of the unexpected victories, the deep and daunting discoveries, and more. In short, I would live my life while it was still mine to live; and fear no evil, not even the shadow of my own death. And I would try to love somebody, because love... love is the only freedom. Love is the only freedom... Love is... freedom. Freedom!

Author's Letter

Dear Reader:

In writing this book, I was not unmindful of the fact that there would be those who doubted the veracity of my narrative. With this in mind, I've tried very hard to confine myself to writing only about those things that could be substantiated through court documents, witness statements, or corroborated recollections. To the extent possible, these things have been compiled for presentation on my Web site at www.keithlamar.org. Unlike the State, who did everything within their considerable power to hide and deprive the public of the truth, my goal has been to bring to light those things that have been kept too long in the dark. Do I believe this book will help save my life? I don't know; but hopefully, if you've read between the lines, it will help save yours.

To say that the criminal justice system is racist and unjust is to state the obvious. A black person who takes the life of a white person is 13.35 times more likely to receive the death penalty than a white person who murders a black. And while black people only make up 12.6% of this nation's population, we constitute a whopping 41.83% of the over 3,100 inmates on death row.[18] But these numbers tell only part of the story.

According to numbers recently released by the Sentencing Project, the United States now has more of its citizens in prison or under some other form of government supervision than any other nation in the world. To put this in perspective, the U.S. now has nine times more people

---

[18] http://www.deathpenaltyinfo.org/race-death-row-inmates-executed-1976

incarcerated (per 100,000) than South Africa during Apartheid, and close to twice the number incarcerated than Stalin's Soviet Union. In response to the growing social ills that plague society—poverty, unemployment, inequality, high rates of crime, etc.—the United States, the freest and most powerful nation in the world, has decided that locking people up and throwing away the keys is the solution.

If you are poor and subject to the prevailing patterns of racism and discrimination, the prospect of someone in your family going to prison is more likely than not. In fact, if you are a black person reading this, nine times out of ten your life has already been affected by having a loved one behind bars. Therefore, the most crucial point to ponder as you consider my case, and what should or should not happen to me, is whether or not prison is a place where people go to be rehabilitated or disposed of.

Let me remind you: there was no evidence linking me to ANY of the crimes that occurred during the Lucasville Uprising. The only evidence—if you can call it that—that was presented in my case came from the testimony of the actual perpetrators of those crimes. This is a fact. So, again, if the State is successful in their efforts to murder me, it won't be because I'm actually guilty and deserve to die; it'll be because they were correct in assuming that no one would care enough to get involved.

In closing, I want to thank each and every one of you for taking the time to read this book. At times, it has been the most rewarding and most painful undertaking I have ever experienced. I turn now to the completion of my autobiography, *Straight Ahead*. No matter what happens in the coming months, my goal is to keep moving forward, even though (in the words of Langston Hughes):

I been scared and battered.
My hopes the wind done scattered.
Snow has friz me,
Sun has baked me,

Looks like between 'em they done
Tried to make me

Stop laughin', stop lovin', stop livin'—
But I don't care!
I'm still here!

Your Brother,

Bomani Shakur
January 2014

Postscript

The oral arguments went forward as planned in December of 2014, and there was a standing-room-only crowd in attendance. People from all over the country came to bear witness, a fact that still humbles me. Unfortunately, the courts ultimately ruled against me, moving my case one step closer to execution. To hear the proceedings in their entirety, please go to:

www.keithlamar.org.

Supporters marching downtown Cincinnati to reach the courthouse where oral arguments would be heard in my case

Also of note is the fact that Kate and David finally recused themselves, and the courts appointed new counsel who, upon request, were granted the long-sought after discovery that I was previously deprived of. This proves that had Kate and David done their due diligence, I likely would have received this material when it mattered most, when my case could have still been put on hold and my attorneys given an opportunity to comb the Prosecutor's files. In terms of my legal chances, I have always been in treacherous waters, rowing against the current, but at least I was inside the lifeboat with a fighting chance. When Kate and David refused to do their job, and the courts denied my final appeal, I was thrown overboard and am now treading water, hoping for a miracle. It's impossible to say at this point what, if anything, will come of being granted discovery at this late date; nevertheless, I remain hopeful. Please keep me in your prayers.

–KL
November 2017

Acknowledgments

In the crossing over
to the other side
of our stumbled glory,
will misty eyes
perceive the pride
of a humble story?
Or will the vacancy
of wisdom faded
echo the confusion
of knowledge forsaken
and ambitions jaded
by ego's illusions?

—Da'im

When people find out that I have been in solitary confinement for the past 20 years, the first question they ask is: "How have you survived for so long without losing your mind?"

It's a good question, one that I've often asked myself over the years. And the answer is: I have not traveled this journey alone. I have always had the love and support of my family and friends who have been with me through thick and thin, encouraging me, guiding me, and loving me. I owe everything to them. Indeed, when I was found guilty of these crimes and ultimately sentenced to death, it was 12 strangers who decided that I deserved to die. However, my family and friends decided otherwise. They decided that I deserved to live, and that's exactly what I've been doing, albeit vicariously, through them.

Carolyn LaMar Dailey

Harriet Brooks

I never knew my father; but my mother's brother, Dwight LaMar (or "Uncle Mannie" as he is called), has been a father figure to me. He has been with me through some very trying times, and I have to pause to acknowledge him for that, for the love and for the strength that his presence has provided in my life. Thank you, Uncle Mannie, for being here with me. I don't know what I would have done without you. I don't even want to imagine it.

I also have to thank my loving aunts, Harriet Brooks and Carolyn LaMar Dailey, who sometimes argue about which one of them loves me the most (smile). In the most sincere truth, I love you both equally and honestly. Both of you have fed me, clothed me, and loved me as if I was your own son, which I am very proud to be.

Dwight LaMar

Kathy LaMar

Princess LaMar

Mona and Nelson LaMar

And to my own mother, Kathy LaMar, I thank you for giving me this life and for bearing the pain of my birth. I know it hasn't always been easy to hold on to each other, but I feel you always moving through my veins, in my blood, flowing straight to my heart. I love you.

To my sister, Princess, I love you very much. You've done an excellent job of raising my niece, and I can't say enough about how beautiful and intelligent she is. It's all a reflection of you, of course. I hope that my being away for all of these years has not made you believe that I don't love you like a big brother should. I do, I do—lord knows it's true. Congratulations on the wedding. I'm wishing you all the best, baby.

To my brother, Nelson (Tut), I simply want to say, "I love you, man." My heart is very glad that you made it through the darkness and found your way to a better life. God bless you and your beautiful wife (my sister), Mona.

I love you, granddad. Thanks for everything you gave me. I see it so clearly now. (smile)

My granddad, Harry LaMar

Tyrone Brooks

Kevin & Mona Lowery
Kayla & Little Kevin

Ken Wright

I want to thank my cousin, Tyrone Brooks, for staying true and for giving me the confidence of knowing that blood is, indeed, thicker than water. You've been more than a brother to me; you've been a friend (one of the best), and I want to thank you for that. I love you.

Speaking of best friends, I would be remiss if I didn't mention my cousin, Kevin Lowery, who has been a constant source of love and light in my life. Few are the ones who keep their childhood promises, but we pricked our fingers and held them together when we were kids and promised to be "blood brothers 'til the end," and you've kept that promise. Thank you for bringing my niece and nephew, Kayla and Little Kevin, into my life and for allowing me to love your wife, Mona, as my sister. After I was sentenced to death, you decided to go to law school and become a lawyer and promised to get me out. Well, though you've only recently graduated, I need you to hurry up and pass the Bar exam. Time is of the essence. Chop-chop!

A special debt of gratitude is owed to my childhood friend, Ken Wright, for standing by me and for always being a positive influence in my life. I've never told you this, but I look up to you, my friend. You have always been the standard by which I've gauged my forward motion. Wherever you are, that's where I want to be, my man. God bless you.

To my little brother André Reid: I want you to know that I love you with all my heart, man. From the alpha to the omega, you will always be my... ALWAYS!

Leon Dailey

Sherita LaMar

Ron Mitchell

Ebony LaMar

My niece, Angel

I want to thank my uncle, Leon Dailey, for always keeping it real with me. You've always treated me like a man, even when I was just a boy, and I thank you for that. I'm definitely a man now and that's a fact, Jack. I love you, Uncle Leon.

To my cousin, Sherita LaMar, thank you for sticking by me when I came to prison, and now you're a grown woman with a son of your own. It's crazy how time flies! Just know that it has meant everything to have you in my life. I'm wishing you and your son all good things. It's not fair for us to have favorites, but you are my favorite. I love you, Rita Dee.

I want to thank my cousin, Ron Mitchell, for coming to sit with me. I love you, Cuz, and I always have. I'm glad you love me as well.

To my niece, Angel, thank you for acknowledging me as your uncle, even though circumstances have prevented me from being in your life. One of my deepest regrets is not being able to show you how much I love you. But make no mistake, you are very dear to me and the love I have for you is larger than life itself. True. You are such a beautiful young woman, and I am exceptionally proud to be your uncle. Your future is so bright that it burns my eyes. Shine, baby, and always remember that you are a voice in this world.

To my sweet baby, Ebony, you know I love you with all my heart, little honey. I always have and I always will. And I want you to always know that no matter how far away I go, you will always, always, always, be near and dear to me.

K. Robert Toy   Herman Carson

Staughton Lynd   Alice Lynd

Da'im

I want to thank Herman Carson, the attorney who went above and beyond the call of duty to preserve my rights. I appreciate everything you've done and continue to do to help me preserve my life. Thank you for sharing your family with me when I was too far away from my own. I love you for that, my friend. I love you, too, Becca. I can't believe you are a mother now, but I know you will be a good one, just as you have been a good sister and friend. I love you.

Robert Toy, thank you for standing up and fighting so hard for me during my trial. It really meant a lot to me. Thank you and God bless you.

To my good friend Darlene Crowl (or "Maggie" as I call her), I want you to know that having you in my life during those most difficult days means everything to me. Not only were you a good investigator, you were a good friend. I can't thank you enough for loving me and for giving me your support when I needed it most. I love you and I'm wishing you all the best, always. Your adopted son, Keith

I want to thank Alice and Staughton Lynd for helping me hold on to my humanity by blessing me with the gift of their love, guidance, and dedication. More than anybody, they have fought alongside me (and on my behalf), when the only thing they stood to gain was the off-chance that my life would somehow be better. I owe them a great debt of gratitude. At a time when they should have been enjoying their "golden years," they have been knee-deep in the "trenches" with me. Thank you, my friends, for loving me unconditionally and for doing so much to change the conditions of my life. I love you.

Let me not forget my brother Da'im, the man who planted the most important seeds in me. I thank whatever gods may be that I met you when I did. You saved me, brah. You helped guide me to my highest self and, through that connection, I found my voice. This book is a reflection of your investment in me. Not everybody can take credit for saving someone's life, but never doubt the depth of the impact you've had on mine. Everybody who knows me, knows your name. Much love and respect to you, my brother.

Anise Marshall

Jackie McMeeking

Paul Gordiejew

I'm also very blessed and thankful to count Anise Marshall among my friends. You are a good sister and I love you. Thank you for your support.

I also need to thank Jackie McMeeking, my friend from England, who has been such an important part of my life these past eight years or so. I want to thank you for investing so much in me. Through the now countless books you've sent me over the years, I've been able to obtain a top-notch education. I can't thank you enough for that and for your friendship. As you frequently remind me, it's amazing that, given all the differences in our upbringing and overall stations in life, we've been able to become such good friends. But that just goes to show that the thing that really makes us who we are transcends age, culture and our own personal biographies. We are spiritual beings, and you've taught me that the only thing that is really required in life is the courage to be honest. Thanks for always telling me the truth and for loving me. I love you very much!

To the students from the *Prison Experiences* anthropology class at Youngstown State University, I owe you guys a great debt of gratitude for reading the manuscript and having the courage to express what it made you think and feel. May each of you find a future that's worthy of your talent and potential, and may you discover that "thing" that brings you happiness. And to Dr. Paul Gordiejew, thank you for having the courage and vision to create the curriculum that allowed your students to interact with us; it was a very rewarding experience. If a new world is possible, it will only come through the efforts, compassion, and understanding of the next generation. Good luck and God bless you all!

Bilge Firat-O'Hearn   Denis O'Hearn

Bobby Gentile

Denis O'Hearn is my comrade, the big brother I never had but always needed. As he mentions in the foreword to this book, he and I met each other by chance. Staughton Lynd sent me his book, *Nothing but an Unfinished Song*, about the Irish hunger striker, Bobby Sands. It was the most important book I've ever read; it saved my life. What do I mean by that? Well, at the time Denis' book found its way into my life, I hadn't touched my family in almost 15 years. In fact, I hadn't touched virtually anything—human, animal or plant—and quite frankly, I was beginning to lose my grip on life. Somehow I found a point of connection in reading about Bobby Sands, and it gave me the push I needed to regain my sense of agency. In 2011, Jason Robb, Siddique Abdullah Hasan, and I went on hunger strike and eventually won the right to touch our friends and family again. The pictures you see are the result of Denis O'Hearn's book. Thank you, Denis, for being such an inspiration in my life—and not just you, but also your wife Bilge Firat-O'Hearn as well. I count you among my closest friends.

I would like to thank my friend, Bobby Gentile, for all he has done to help me to stay spiritually strong. You've been there through some of my darkest days and I thank you for not giving up on me. God bless you and your family.

To the rest of my friends and family: Felicia, Tyreese, Maurice (RIP, brah), Dude (Get it together, man!), Aunt Kathy, Lil' Man, Veronica, Uncle Clarkie, Grama Dee, Aunt Marcia, Phyllis, Brock, Angela, Torean, Rakaya, Hasson, Tyrone Gilbert, Wayne, Bruce, Lil' Moe, Bob Ford, Eric, Dame, Topcat, Buddy, Troy—I love each and every one of you. If I neglected to mention your name, please charge it to my head, not my heart; I'm living under strain.

Back Row, L-R: Staughton Lynd, D Jones,
                Annabelle Parker, Kunta Kenyatta
Front Row, L-R: Natural, Ben Turk, Laurie Hoover

Ben Turk

Kate Pleuss   Weslie Coleman

Lorry Swain   Eric O'Neil

Thanks to my young friend, Beth Atim, for your positivity. You are a special little woman and I'm glad to call you my friend.

I want to thank the group of supporters who, without pay or significant recognition, have kept the story about the Lucasville Uprising alive. I want to thank, in no particular order:

• Kunta Kenyatta and his wife, Laurie Hoover.

• Kate Pleuss, Weslie Coleman and Ben Turk for taking the time to find out about my (our) struggle. I really appreciate all that you three have done to make the case for a better world, one that thrives without the need for prisons. Let's continue to work toward that vision.

• D Jones and his wife, Natural. I'm constantly praying for Legacy and his speedy recovery. How humbling it was to know that while your young son's life hung in the balance you still came out to support us on the 20th anniversary of the uprising.

• Annabelle Parker, my friend from the Netherlands. I thank you for all the hard work and effort you made to get the word out. I love you.

• Eric O'Neil and Lorry Swain for keeping up the fight to end the death penalty and for insisting that a better, braver world is possible. I believe it.

• Bob Fitrakis and Suzanne Patzer for allowing me to use your radio show to publicize my plight and bring people up to speed with the current status of our collective legal situations as they stand in the courts.

Sharon Danann

Abdul Qahhar

Printess Williams

Greg Curry

• Sharon Danann. Thank you for everything. It really means a lot to have you by my side.

• Abdul Qahhar. You are an inspiration and a true representation of righteousness, steadfastness, and commitment to the cause. May I one day walk in your shoes, never ceasing and always reaching for higher heights. Love you, brah.

• And to all the people around the country and the world who lent your love, energy, and support to us during the hunger strike, I think it's safe for me to speak for the other guys when I say we very much appreciated your care and concern, and we look forward to collaborating with you in the future. Thank you and power to the people!

To my little brother, Printess, may you always know your worth and continue to trust in the purpose of your life. We came by it (the knowledge) the "hard way," but that by no means diminishes the depth of what we were given. "Life is real/love is true/as long as we do what we gotta do." Remember? Stay vibrant, man. Keep looking for that deeper thing. It's there for you...

To my brother and comrade, Greg Curry, I couldn't have asked for a more loyal and trusted travel companion—and what a trip it's been. I love you, man, and that's from the bottom of my heart, real talk. We met when I was 18 years old, and you embraced me and assumed the role as "big brah," and I'm thankful you did. I can't even begin to tell you how grateful I am for the strength and confidence that having you in my life has instilled in me. It ain't over, man. It ain't never over!!

Jason Robb

Siddique Abdullah Hasan

Namir Abdul Mateen

George Skatzes

To Jason Robb, It's been a real pleasure getting to know you, man; you are a riddle wrapped up in a conundrum. Thanks for all the help and guidance, my friend. You are a good man and it's been a definite plus having you along for the ride. Stay strong, stay true, and always be you. Ya feel me?

To my brother and comrade, Hasan: What a journey it has been, huh? I will always remember the kindness you've shown me over these years, man. A scholar and gentleman—that's what you are. Thanks for taking the time to peruse the manuscript; you caught a lot of stuff. Stay on that "straight path," man, as I know you will.

To Namir Abdul Mateen: yeah, it's true, I tell you. No doubt about that, brah. I can't imagine what this trip would have been like without your constant laughter and compassion. I love you, man. —Your "Little Brother"

To George Skatzes, I just want to say thank you for the kindness you showed me during our time at Mansfield and for taking the time to make me feel included. And for always cultivating a sense of solidarity among us. We haven't been around each other these past several years, but you have always been close at heart. Stay strong. Keep your hope alive.

To my comrades behind bars, the ones who refuse to be counted among the broken ones—Gary "G-Rilla" Roberts, Big Heady, 'Pone, Nati, Askari, Young Tek, De'Angelo, Pook, Len Bob, Devo, Amadi, Blood Cunningham, Chino, Eric Scales, and all the rest—stay strong my brothers and remember: nothing comes to a sleeper but a dream.

Amy Gordiejew

My little friend, Lola

My little friend, Daniel

Last, but not least, I would like to thank my friend, Amy Gordiejew, without whom this book would not have been possible. Even though we've only been in each other's lives for a short period of time, I feel like I've known you forever. This project has been frustrating at times, I know, but you've shown the utmost patience and perseverance and I can't thank you enough for that. Thank you for sharing your beautiful children, Daniel and Lola, with me and for trusting me enough to let me love and hug them. I can't tell you how much that has meant to me. I want to thank your whole family for allowing me to take up so much of your time. I have no idea if what we've done together will change the direction of my life, but having you in my life has changed the direction of my aspirations. I owe you so much for encouraging me and for putting in so much work to help me finish this project. We did it! I love you.

In closing, I just want to say that life is short and full of mysteries, and the most fundamental fact of our existence is that life is not fair. Still, in the end, what matters most is not the struggles we endure and conquer, but the friends we've made and loved along the way.

Appendix I

CLAIMS ENTITLING KEITH LAMAR
TO WRIT OF HABEAS CORPUS[19]

FIRST CLAIM FOR RELIEF
THE SUPPRESSION BY THE PROSECUTION OF EVIDENCE FAVORABLE TO AN ACCUSED VIOLATES DUE PROCESS WHERE THE EVIDENCE IS MATERIAL TO GUILT OR PUNISHMENT. BRADY V. MARYLAND (1963) 373 U.S. 83; KYLES V. WHITLEY (1995), 514 U.S. 419.

SECOND CLAIM FOR RELIEF
THE DUE PROCESS CLAUSE OF THE FEDERAL CONSTITUTION ENTITLES AN ACCUSED TO TRIAL BEFORE AN IMPARTIAL JUDGE.

THIRD CLAIM FOR RELIEF
KEITH LAMAR WAS SELECTIVELY PROSECUTED FOR THIS OFFENSE AND THE ONLY INMATE CHARGED WITH A CAPITAL OFFENSE FOR KILLINGS OF INMATES ALONE {NOT A PRISON GUARD} THEREBY DENYING MR. LAMAR HIS CONSTITUTIONAL RIGHTS UNDER THE FIFTH AND FOURTEENTH AMENDMENTS TO THE U.S. CONSTITUTION. MR. LAMAR WAS DENIED THE OPPORTUNITY TO FULLY DEVELOP THIS CLAIM DUE TO THE ACTIONS OF THE STATE AND THE COURT.

FOURTH CLAIM FOR RELIEF
KEITH LAMAR WAS DENIED HIS RIGHT TO A FAIR TRIAL AS, GUARANTEED BY THE UNITED STATES CONSTITUTION,

---

[19] Case: 1:04-cv-00541-TMR-MRM Doc#: 19, Filed: 08/16/04 in the United States District Court for the Southern District of Ohio

WHEN THE TRIAL COURT REFUSED TO SEVER THE WEAVER COUNT FROM THE REMAINING CHARGES EVEN THOUGH THEY OCCURRED AT DIFFERENT TIMES AND UNDER DIFFERENT CIRCUMSTANCES.

FIFTH CLAIM FOR RELIEF
WHEN A TRIAL COURT UNREASONABLY AND ARBITRARILY RESTRICTS A DEFENDANT'S VOIR DIRE EXAMINATION, PREJUDICIAL ERROR OCCURS IN THAT THE DEFENDANT IS DENIED THE RIGHT TO A FAIR AND IMPARTIAL JURY IN VIOLATION OF THE SIXTH AND FOURTEENTH AMENDMENTS TO THE UNITED STATES CONSTITUTION.

SIXTH CLAIM FOR RELIEF
MR. LAMAR WAS DENIED HIS RIGHT TO A FAIR AND IMPARTIAL JURY WHEN THE TRIAL COURT FAILED TO EXCUSE A JUROR WHO WAS AN "AUTOMATIC DEATH PENALTY JUROR," THEREBY VIOLATING THE SIXTH AND FOURTEENTH AMENDMENTS TO THE UNITED STATES CONSTITUTION.

SEVENTH CLAIM FOR RELIEF
THE TRIAL COURT ERRONEOUSLY ALLOWED THE PROSECUTING ATTORNEY TO USE HIS PEREMPTORY CHALLENGES TO EXCLUDE THE ONLY TWO AFRICAN-AMERICAN JURORS ON MR. LAMAR'S VENIRE. THIS VIOLATED THE SIXTH AND FOURTEENTH AMENDMENTS TO THE UNITED STATES CONSTITUTION.

EIGHTH CLAIM FOR RELIEF
ADMISSION OF GRUESOME AND MISLEADING PHOTOS WHEN THEIR PREJUDICIAL EFFECT OUTWEIGHS THEIR PROBATIVE VALUE DENYS PETITIONER A FAIR TRIAL, DUE PROCESS AND A RELIABLE DETERMINATION OF HIS GUILT

AND SENTENCE AS GUARANTEED BY THE FIFTH, SIXTH, EIGHTH AND FOURTEENTH AMENDMENTS TO THE UNITED STATES CONSTITUTION.

NINTH CLAIM FOR RELIEF
THE ADMISSION OF HIGHLY PREJUDICIAL HEARSAY EVIDENCE IN VIOLATION OF THE OHIO EVIDENCE RULES DENYS PETITIONER HIS FEDERAL CONSTITUTIONAL RIGHTS TO A FAIR TRIAL AND HIS RIGHT TO CROSS-EXAMINE WITNESSES AGAINST HIM.

TENTH CLAIM FOR RELIEF
AS A MATTER OF LAW, THERE IS INSUFFICIENT EVIDENCE TO CONVICT PETITIONER OF MANY OF THE CHARGES THEREBY DENYING THE PETITIONER DUE PROCESS OF LAW.

ELEVENTH CLAIM FOR RELIEF
THE TRIAL COURT ERRED IN ALLOWING THE ADMISSION OF EVIDENCE OF UNCHARGED OTHER ACTS BY THE DEFENDANT.

TWELFTH CLAIM FOR RELIEF
A CAPITAL DEFENDANT IS DENIED HIS RIGHTS TO A FAIR TRIAL, DUE PROCESS AND A RELIABLE DETERMINATION OF HIS GUILT AND SENTENCE AS GUARANTEED BY THE FIFTH, SIXTH, EIGHTH AND FOURTEENTH AMENDMENTS TO THE UNITED STATES CONSTITUTION WHEN THE PROSECUTOR REPEATEDLY ENGAGES IN IMPROPER ARGUMENT AND OTHER MISCONDUCT PRIOR TO AND THROUGHOUT THE TRIAL.

THIRTEENTH CLAIM FOR RELIEF
THE TRIAL COURT ERRED IN FAILING TO GRANT A MISTRIAL, OR IN THE ALTERNATIVE, TO DISMISS THE JURY WHEN THE PROSECUTOR REPEATEDLY ARGUED INAPPROPRIATELY

REGARDING MITIGATING FACTORS WHICH ACTED TO DENY MR. LAMAR THE INDIVIDUALIZED SENTENCING DETERMINATION REQUIRED BY THE FIFTH, SIXTH, EIGHTH, AND FOURTEENTH AMENDMENTS TO THE U.S. CONSTITUTION.

FOURTEENTH CLAIM FOR RELIEF
IT IS PREJUDICIAL ERROR TO ADMIT ALL EVIDENCE SUBMITTED BY THE STATE IN THE GUILT-INNOCENCE PHASE INTO THE MITIGATION PHASE WHEN MUCH OF THE EVIDENCE WAS NOT RELEVANT TO ANY SPECIFIC AGGRAVATING CIRCUMSTANCE. SUCH ERROR DENIED KEITH LAMAR HIS RIGHTS UNDER THE FIFTH, SIXTH, EIGHTH AND FOURTEENTH AMENDMENTS TO THE U.S. CONSTITUTION.

FIFTEENTH CLAIM FOR RELIEF
THE TRIAL COURT ERRED IN INSTRUCTING THE JURY DURING THE SENTENCING PHASE BY (A) FAILING TO INFORM THE JURY A SOLITARY JUROR COULD PREVENT THE DEATH SENTENCE AND (B) IN PLACING UNDUE INFLUENCE ON THE REQUIREMENT OF UNANIMITY SUCH THAT MR. LAMAR'S DEATH SENTENCES LACK THE RELIABILITY REQUIRED BY THE EIGHTH AND FOURTEENTH AMENDMENTS TO THE U.S. CONSTITUTION.

SIXTEENTH CLAIM FOR RELIEF
REPEATEDLY INSTRUCTING THAT A JURY'S VERDICT IS ONLY A RECOMMENDATION VIOLATES THE FIFTH, EIGHTH AND FOURTEENTH AMENDMENTS TO THE U. S. CONSTITUTION. THE PREJUDICE A PETITIONER SUFFERS FROM THIS CONSTITUTIONAL VIOLATION IS FURTHER EXACERBATED BY USING THE TERM 'RECOMMENDATION' ON THE ACTUAL VERDICT FORMS.

SEVENTEENTH CLAIM FOR RELIEF

THE TRIAL COURT FAILED TO INSTRUCT THE JURY THAT IT MUST MAKE A FINDING ON THE ALTERNATIVE THEORIES ON THE FELONY MURDER SPECIFICATION THUS VIOLATING THE FOURTEENTH AMENDMENT TO THE UNITED STATES CONSTITUTION.

EIGHTEENTH CLAIM FOR RELIEF

WHEN A CAPITAL DEFENDANT IS CHARGED AND CONVICTED UNDER ALTERNATIVE THEORIES OF AGGRAVATED MURDER PURSUANT TO OHIO REV. CODE ANN. SECTION 2903.01, HE MAY ONLY BE SENTENCED ON ONE OF THE COUNTS. THE OTHER COUNT IS VACATED.

NINETEENTH CLAIM FOR RELIEF

TRIAL COUNSEL'S PERFORMANCE FELL BELOW THE PREVAILING PROFESSIONAL NORMS THEREBY VIOLATING MR. LAMAR'S RIGHT TO THE EFFECTIVE ASSISTANCE OF COUNSEL.

TWENTIETH CLAIM FOR RELIEF

THE TRIAL COURT ERRED WHEN IT FAILED TO COMPLY WITH THE DICTATES OF R.C. 2929.03 BY WEIGHING NON-STATUTORY AGGRAVATING CIRCUMSTANCES, BY RELYING ON EVIDENCE THAT WAS NOT A PART OF THE RECORD, BY DISCOUNTING THE MITIGATING FACTORS AND BY FAILING TO ARTICULATE THE REASONS WHY THE AGGRAVATING CIRCUMSTANCES THE OFFENDER WAS FOUND GUILTY OF COMMITTING WERE SUFFICIENT TO OUTWEIGH THE MITIGATING FACTORS. THIS FAILURE DENIED THE PETITIONER HIS DUE PROCESS RIGHTS AS GUARANTEED BY THE UNITED STATES CONSTITUTION.

TWENTY FIRST CLAIM FOR RELIEF
EVIDENCE THAT HAS BEEN UNCOVERED SINCE THE TRIAL OF THIS CASE, AND PRESENTED TO THE TRIAL COURT BY WAY OF A NEW TRIAL MOTION, INDICATE THAT MR. LAMAR IS "ACTUALLY INNOCENT" OF MANY OF THE CHARGES AGAINST HIM AND TO LEAVE HIS CONVICTIONS AND SENTENCES IN TACT WOULD VIOLATE HIS CONSTITUTIONAL RIGHTS TO DUE PROCESS, A FAIR TRIAL, EFFECTIVE ASSISTANCE OF COUNSEL AND A RELIABLE SENTENCING DETERMINATION AS GUARANTEED BY THE FIFTH, SIXTH, EIGHTH, AND FOURTEENTH AMENDMENTS TO THE U.S CONSTITUTION.

TWENTY SECOND CLAIM FOR RELIEF
APPELLATE COUNSEL WAS INEFFECTIVE IN THEIR REPRESENTATION BY FAILING TO PRESENT ALL MERITORIOUS ISSUES FOR APPEAL, THEREBY VIOLATING MR. LAMAR'S RIGHT TO THE EFFECTIVE ASSISTANCE OF APPELLATE COUNSEL AS GUARANTEED BY THE EIGHTH AND FOURTEENTH AMENDMENTS TO THE UNITED STATES CONSTITUTION.

TWENTY THIRD CLAIM FOR RELIEF
OHIO APP.R. 26(B), ON ITS FACE AND AS APPLIED TO KEITH LAMAR DENIED MR. LAMAR DUE PROCESS AND EQUAL PROTECTION OF THE LAW AS GUARANTEED BY THE FIFTH, SIXTH, EIGHTH, NINTH, AND FOURTEENTH AMENDMENTS TO THE CONSTITUTION OF THE UNITED STATES.

TWENTY FOURTH CLAIM FOR RELIEF
THE FIFTH, EIGHTH AND FOURTEENTH AMENDMENTS TO THE UNITED STATES CONSTITUTION GUARANTEE A CONVICTED CAPITAL DEFENDANT A FAIR AND IMPARTIAL REVIEW OF HIS DEATH SENTENCE. THE STATUTORILY

MANDATED PROPORTIONALITY PROCESS IN OHIO DOES NOT COMPORT WITH THIS CONSTITUTIONAL REQUIREMENT AND THUS IS FATALLY FLAWED.

TWENTY FIFTH CLAIM FOR RELIEF

THE FIFTH, SIXTH, EIGHTH AND FOURTEENTH AMENDMENTS TO THE UNITED STATES CONSTITUTION ESTABLISH THE REQUIREMENTS FOR A VALID DEATH PENALTY SCHEME. R.C. 2903.01, 2929.02, 2929.021, 2903.022, 2929.023, 2929.03, 2929.04 AND 2929.05, OHIO'S STATUTORY PROVISIONS GOVERNING THE IMPOSITION OF THE DEATH PENALTY, DO NOT MEET THE PRESCRIBED CONSTITUTIONAL REQUIREMENTS AND ARE UNCONSTITIONAL, BOTH ON THEIR FACE AND AS APPLIED.

Appendix II

SUMMARIES AND TRANSCRIPTS OF WITNESS STATEMENTS

Judge Dlott (Hasan's district court judge) granted:
"Upon request, access to the interview summaries and transcripts still maintained by the OSHP at their facilities at Alum Creek Dr., Columbus, Ohio."

a. When directed by the trial court before trial, counsel for the State made available to Counsel for LaMar the names of 43 prisoners who had been interviewed by the OSHP. Separately, the State made available a list of database entries, but, with the acquiescence of the trial court judge, refused to say which prisoners had been interviewed for each database entry.

The 43 names did not include five of the six prisoner witnesses subsequently called by the prosecution at trial. The database entries after the following interviews with the prosecution witnesses have never been made available to LaMar's defense counsel:

Robert Bass—Interviews on 05/18/93; 12/02/93; 01/06/94; 03/31/94; 07/14/94; and 10/24/94.

Michael Childers—Interviews on 05/04/93; 05/05/93; 07/01/93; 10/26/93; and 07/20/94.

Stacey Gordon—Interviews on 05/26/93; 09/08/94 (when Gordon testified on the occasion of his plea agreement that he did not know LaMar and had not seen LaMar in L-6 on April 11); 12/07/94; 01/05/95; 01/26/95; 02/09/95; and 10/25/95.

John Malveaux—Interviews on 04/29/93; 10/26/93, and 03/03/94.

Ricky Rutherford—Interviews on 05/05/93; 10/26/93 (two interviews); and 08/02/94.

b. The State has never made available the following material, itemized in the foregoing listing, concerning critical witnesses who were with LaMar in the cell on K-side at the time Dennis Weaver was murdered:

William Bowling—The State has never made available transcripts of the following taped interviews with Bowling: 04/29/93, Tape A071; 10/26/93, Tape A180; and 08/04/94, Tape D057. Additionally, the State has not produced the database entries summarizing these interviews. The State has also never made available the database entries of an additional, untaped interview with Bowling on 05/10/93, and a second, untaped interview on 10/26/93.

DEPOSITIONS

Counsel for LaMar have received no audio or video tapes of any of the following depositions:

Copies of any audio or video depositions of each of the witnesses who testified at Petitioner's trial:

Robert Bass, 03/31/94, Interview #1230, Tape D054

Michael Childers, 07/28/94, Interview #1303, Tape D055

Lewis Jones, 04/08/94, Interview #1334, Tape D051

John Malveaux, 03/03/94, Interview #1205, Tape D066

Ricky Rutherford, 08/02/94, Interview #1302, Tape D056

OTHER DEPOSITIONS

Copies of any audio or videotapes prepared by the special prosecutor or the OSHP during the Lucasville Investigation relevant to the murder for which the Defendant has been convicted:

Stanley Aldridge, 12/13/93, Interview #1083, Tape D015; and 01/21/94, Interview #1146, Tape D002.

Daniel Belcher, 05/04/94, Interview #1257, Tape D032

William Bowling, 08/04/94, Interview #1301, Tape D057

Ruben Brazzile, 02/04/94, Interview #1183, Tape D035

Donald Cassell, 07/21/94, Interview #1338, Tape D067

Hiawatha Frezzell, CD 02/11/94, Interview #1178, Tape D065

Daniel Johnson, 06/08/94, Interview #1269, Tape D031

Gerald Kelly, Interview #1155, Tape D023

David Lomonche, CD 05/19/94, Interview #1330, Tape D030

Steven Macko, 05/05/94, Interview #1255, Tape D036

Brian Seneff, 12/14/93, Interview #1151, Tape D025

Thomas Taylor, 03/14/94, Interview #1217, Tape D52

Reginald Williams, 05/06/94, Interview #1253A, Tape D033